BUDO TAIJUTSU

AN ILLUSTRATED REFERENCE GUIDE OF
BUJINKAN DOJO BUDO TAIJUTSU

DUNCAN MITCHELL

BUDŌ DŌKŌKAI (BRISBANE, AUSTRALIA)

Disclaimer: This book is presented as a reference guide only. Nothing described in this book should be practiced or undertaken without the personal guidance of a suitably qualified and experienced martial arts instructor. Furthermore, a physician should be first consulted before deciding whether or not to attempt any of the techniques described. The author and publisher accept no responsibility whatsoever for any injury that may result from practicing the techniques and/or instructions within. This book is presented only as a means of preserving a unique aspect of the heritage of the martial arts and neither the author or publisher makes any representation, guarantee or warrantee that any technique or instruction described within will be safe or effective in any self-defence situation. In addition, specific martial arts techniques detailed in these pages may not be justified in any particular situation or applicable under local, state or federal laws. Neither the publisher or the author makes any representation or warranty regarding the legality or appropriateness of any technique mentioned in this book.

Written and Illustrated by Duncan Mitchell

Edited by Benjamin Düster

Published by the Budō Dōkōkai, Brisbane Australia.

www.budodokokai.com

ISBN 978-0-6489608-0-5 (paperback)

ISBN 978-0-6489608-1-2 (ebook)

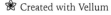 Created with Vellum

For Yoshie

CONTENTS

PART II
KEIKO GATA (PRACTICE FORMS)

KIHON GATA

SHINDEN FUDŌ RYŪ DAKENTAIJUTSU

KUKISHIN RYŪ DAKENTAIJUTSU

TAKAGI YOSHIN RYŪ JŪTAIJUTSU

GYOKKO RYŪ KOSSHIJUTSU

KOTŌ RYŪ KOPPŌJUTSU

TOGAKURE RYŪ NINPŌ TAIJUTSU

ACKNOWLEDGMENTS

This book is a culmination of five years' work, and in the process, I find myself owing a great debt of gratitude to all those who provided their help and support in completing this project.

Firstly, I wish to thank the teachers and senior students of the Bujinkan under whose personal guidance I was able to gain insight into Budō Taijutsu. In particular I wish to acknowledge the Bujinkan Sōke (grand-master), Masaaki Hatsumi-sensei for his dedication in passing on his legacy to myself and the many thousands of practitioners worldwide.

Special thanks must go to my teacher and mentor, Isamu Shiraishi-sensei, who tirelessly and personally guided my Budō development over several decades - always with a smile on his face.

I would also like to give mention to my other teachers in Japan - Hosoda-sensei, Sakuma-sensei, Sakai-sensei and the late Seno-sensei. Their patient guidance, instruction and friendship over the many years have made my life so much richer.

For the direct assistance, moral support and encouragement over the course of this project I wish to give special thanks to Peter Cook, Duncan Stewart, Gillian Booth, Warren Cross, Dean Martin, Nathan Anning, Ben Bellamy, Sean Joyce, Rodger McQuitty, Mark Sernia, Mel Arotis, Stephen Wallace and Cid Vieira Jr.

For the advice on writing and early editing on the project, I wish to thank Dave Grant.

For all of his help with notes, honest appraisal, assistance and belief in this project I also give special thanks to Dale Heers.

I wish to acknowledge the work put in by the editor Benjamin Düster, who tirelessly checked and rechecked my manuscript, provided useful notes and kept the project moving forward.

My wife, Yoshie, stood by me throughout the many rewrites, writing binges, research, late nights, early mornings and lost weekends. All this shifted many obligations onto her shoulders, but she supported me throughout. Thank you Yoshie, for your love and support; I can never thank you enough.

Finally, I wish to give a deep bow to the many students of Bujinkan Dōjō Budō Taijutsu throughout the world and their quiet dedication in continuing this art and passing it on to future generations.

Duncan Mitchell,

Brisbane, Australia

OUR LEGACY

The Bujinkan is the martial arts organisation formed by Masaaki Hatsumi-sensei to propagate the essence of the nine Ryūha (traditional schools of martial arts) of which he inherited the title of Sōke (grandmaster).

- 神伝不動流打拳体術 Shinden Fudō Ryū Daken Taijutsu
- 九鬼神伝流八法秘剣術 Kuki Shinden Ryū Happō Biken-Jutsu
- 高木揚心流柔体術 Takagi Yōshin Ryū Jūtai-Jutsu
- 玉虎流骨指術 Gyokko Ryū Kosshi-Jutsu
- 虎倒流骨法術 Kotō Ryū Koppō-Jutsu
- 義鑑流骨法術 Gikan Ryū Koppō-Jutsu
- 玉心流骨法術 Gyokushin Ryū Koppō-Jutsu
- 戸隠流忍法体術 Togakure Ryū Ninpō Taijutsu
- 雲隠流忍法体術 Kumogakure Ryū Ninpō Taijutsu

The Bujinkan has its headquarters in Noda City, Japan and has spread internationally since its formation in 1968; now encompassing thousands of students worldwide.

It is the Bujinkan's training philosophy of moving away from the *form* of techniques and developing one's response in accordance with the situation that brings forth a heightened awareness and a dynamic martial art.

高松寿嗣 Toshitsugu Takamatsu - Teacher of the Bujinkan Founder Masaaki Hatsumi

Toshitsugu Takamatsu was born in 1888 and from the age of nine was schooled daily in the martial arts that he later would inherit as grandmaster.

Initially, he trained in Kōbe under the tutelage of Toda Shinryuken Masamitsu and then in the Dōjō of Mizuta Yoshitaro Tadafusa. Later he moved to the nearby town of Akashi with his father, where he trained under Ishitani Matsutaro Tagekage.

In 1912, Takamatsu travelled to China where he lived until his return to Japan in 1919. In China, he headed the "Nippon Minkoku Seinen Butou-kai" martial arts organisation. He was also involved in many incidents that had him fighting for his life. It was during this period that he became known as Mōko no Tora (The Mongolian Tiger).

In 1957, Takamatsu-sensei took on a young Masaaki Hatsumi as his student and successor. From that point on, Takamatsu-sensei would devote his time through training and writing to pass on the nine schools and his greater vision of Budō to his student.

初見良昭 Masaaki Hatsumi - Bujinkan Founder

Born 1931 in Noda City, Japan, Masaaki Hatsumi-sensei spent his youth training in a number of martial arts amongst which he was highly accomplished in Jūdō (5th Dan), Karate (6th Dan), Kendō (3rd Dan), Aikidō and western boxing.

During the period immediately after the Second World War, he was assigned to teach Jūdō at an American air force base near Tokyo. It was here that he came upon the realisation that, since the Japanese martial arts modernised into competitive sports, the larger and more athletic Americans could achieve in a very short time what would take the smaller Japanese years of study. It was then Hatsumi-sensei set himself to search for the true Japanese martial arts of ancient Japan.

His search led him to a martial artist from Nara in the west of Japan named Toshitsugu Takamatsu.

From his first encounter at age 27, Hatsumi-sensei would regularly take the night train on Saturday evening to arrive Sunday morning for his apprenticeship in the nine martial art lineages he would later inherit as grandmaster. Hatsumi-sensei continued his training for fifteen years until the death of Takamatsu-sensei in 1972.

Combining the essence of the teachings from Takamatsu, Hatsumi-sensei established the Bujinkan Dōjō.

Masaaki Hatsumi has served as an advisor for many movies, television shows and theatre productions since the 1960s such as "Shinobi no Mono", "Kage no Gundan" and "You Only Live Twice". He even had an acting role as "Yamaji Tetzuzan" in the children's TV series "Sekai Ninja-sen Jiraya" (Jiraya and the World Ninja War).

Hatsumi-sensei is the author of many books in both English and Japanese and has produced a series of DVDs demonstrating the martial arts of the Bujinkan.

From 1986 till 2003, he travelled the world conducting seminars where five hundred to a thousand enthusiasts would gather to train together at one time.

Due to his work in spreading the true martial arts of Japan around the world, Masaaki Hatsumi has been given numerous awards, including being the first martial artist to receive the International Culture Award from the emperor of Japan.

INTRODUCTION

For more than thirty years, I have been a member of the Japanese martial arts organisation, the Bujinkan and a student of its grandmaster, Masaaki Hatsumi-sensei.

I would watch Hatsumi-sensei at his Dōjō in wonder at the way he simultaneously controlled the space around him and the balance (both mental and physical) of the people he demonstrated on.

A characteristic of training with Hatsumi-sensei was laughter seeping out from around the room as his students were both perplexed and amazed at how he could take control from an unexpected position, evade a strike in such a way as to leave his opponent *sure* they would hit or have them fly through the air with no sensation of a throwing technique being applied.

Many people look at the light, spontaneous movement of Hatsumi-sensei and believe that our normal training will be of this type, but like any great artisan, the movement of Hatsumi-sensei is a result of decades of arduous training and study. Hatsumi-sensei reminds us that he is instructing at a very high level to the senior teachers in his classes and that all students must *first* establish a strong foundation.

Establishing a strong foundation initially requires a high degree of precision and accuracy in your training.

My purpose in writing this book is to provide both, the new and the experienced student a simple reference guide to the basic techniques and physical mechanics of Bujinkan Dōjō Budō Taijutsu.

Although there are already many excellent books discussing the history, philosophy and high-level training principles of the Bujinkan, my intention is to provide a purely technical guide to the basic techniques, physical mechanics and Kata (forms) of Budō Taijutsu.

This book is based on my years of study with various Japanese teachers and provides access to many of the theoretical concepts and training methods that have, until now, not always been readily available to the Western student of the Bujinkan.

I should point out that this book is not intended to provide shortcuts, 'hacks' or teach you a few tricks to amaze your training partners. Everything written here is only an outline and requires *you* to provide the hard work and study to achieve the outcome you desire.

Furthermore, although I have tried to be as detailed as possible, this book is not intended as a substitute for training in a good Dōjō with a qualified, knowledgeable and experienced teacher – but only as a reference and supplementary training guide for those wishing to go further in their study of Budō Taijutsu.

What is Budō Taijutsu?

Taijutsu (body technique) refers to the way we use our body and implies the use of the whole body in a coordinated manner. By adding the word Budō (martial arts) to the word Taijutsu, we are referring to the way martial artists use their body.

Budō Taijutsu could denote a striking technique, a grappling technique, a sword technique, but more accurately it refers to something beyond techniques – to the physical mechanics of the most efficient use of the human body in the martial arts. Budō Taijutsu is beyond a certain set of techniques, a way of using a sword or staff or a *style* that can be learned.

When you study Budō Taijutsu, you are studying the most natural and efficient way of employing your body and going back to the origin of Budō, before various systems were codified and grouped into individual sets of skills.

However, before we can train in something as conceptual as Budō Taijutsu, we first need to ground ourselves in a training style or technique that we can build off. For the student of the Bujinkan, this means studying the techniques of the nine schools of Kobudō (historical martial arts) that are the basis of the organisation.

How to Use This Book

This book is divided into two parts:

- **Part One is "Foundations of Budō Taijutsu"** which provides a reference to the training principles, physical preparation and basic technique that are the building blocks of Budō Taijutsu.
- **Part Two is "Keiko Gata (Practice Forms)"** is an outline of the basic Kata most commonly practiced in the Bujinkan.

I should make clear that this book is not a translation of the Densho (scrolls of transmission of the secrets for the art), but my description of the basic technique and Kata. In researching this book, I have reviewed original Japanese handwritten documents, books and DVD produced by Hatsumi-sensei, my training notes and study with Japanese teachers over the years.

In writing the Kata, I have outlined the basic forms as simply as I could and avoided nuanced terms, histories, philosophical ideas and differences between the schools.

In the original Densho, often slightly different names are used for techniques that are similar or the same. I have consolidated these as much as I could. There are also often steps or instructions in several Kata that seem out of place and are omitted in actual Dōjō practice; I have also omitted them from the descriptions.

Hatsumi-sensei suggested that Kata should not be read as a set of instructions to follow, but as a story or history retold from one generation to the next. To practice the Kata is to retell the tale and walk for a moment on the path of our ancestors in the art. In keeping with this feeling, I have described each Kata in the first person.

It should be noted that there are sometimes diverse and contradictory interpretations on how basic techniques and Kata are performed between different teachers in Japan. Rather than listing all the contradictory views and variations, I decided to present a singular and standardised version of each technique. It should therefore be noted that this book is only a reference guide and that instruction from your teacher should always take precedence over any description or illustration provided in this book.

The Keiko Gata I have selected for this book were done so on the basis that they have been taught in Japan over the past few decades and have appeared in Hatsumi-sensei's books and DVDs.

I have omitted the following Kata, although they (or aspects of them) *are* practiced by some teachers in the Bujinkan:

- Gikan Ryū Koppō-Jutsu
- Gyokushin Ryū Koppō-Jutsu
- Kumogakure Ryū Ninpō Taijutsu
- Shinden Fudo Ryū Taijutsu (or Jūtaijutsu)
- Kukishin Ryū Shinken Gata Tora no Maki
- Takagi Yoshin Ryū Shoden Ura Kata
- Takagi Yoshin Ryū Ishitani-Den
- Asayama Ichiden Ryū
- Bokuden Ryū Jujutsu

Finally, I would like to express my sincere hope that this book provides you, the reader, with some guidance and direction on the rewarding and lifelong journey in the practice of Japanese Budō.

Please feel free to contact me with any suggestions, corrections and requests for future editions of this book.

Duncan Mitchell

www.budodokokai.com

budodokokai@gmail.com

PART I

FOUNDATIONS OF BUDŌ TAIJUTSU

武道体術の基礎技

1

TRAINING AND ETIQUETTE

稽古と礼法 KEIKO TO REIHŌ

Improvement in Budō Taijutsu requires a great deal of practice. Rather than 'self-discipline', it is preferable to create the natural rhythm of 'habit' that supports your training and can be maintained throughout your life.

生活 Seikatsu (Lifestyle)

A Budōka (martial artist) should live a long and healthy life. Like martial arts techniques, these principles cannot be learnt simply by reading them but need to be practiced again and again.

Stretching and Breathing Exercises for Thirty Minutes Before Sleep.

Practice the basic stretching and breathing exercises as described in "Chapter 2: Physical Preparation" daily. Taking half an hour before you retire to bed each night to stretch promotes a night of deeper and more restful sleep.

Unprocessed Food and Exercise.

Maintain a diet high in vegetables, whole-grains and quality protein while avoiding processed foods with high levels of sugar and salt.

Walking is an important basis for Budō training, and it is important to walk for approximately one to three hours daily. Other exercise including running, swimming, cycling and resistance training is also useful for maintaining fitness and preventing injury.

Respect the Natural World (Of the Shintō Gods and Buddhas).

Respect the natural world, the natural environment and cultivate a spiritual connection to the forces greater than yourself.

Shinrin-Yoku (Forest Bathing) is the practice of spending time in the woods or natural environment and can improve your body's natural resistance to disease which is suppressed under conditions of stress.

Although it may not be possible to visit a small shrine of a temple in the mountains, you should try and spend some time in nature each week.

Avoid Stress and Anxiety.

Stress and anxiety are serious problems and can lead you to be susceptible to severe health conditions. Life is difficult and can throw up many challenges, learn strategies to avoid stress, create boundaries and give yourself time and space to relax.

A diet of unprocessed food, daily exercise, spending time in nature, taking time out for Budō practice and breathing exercises when faced with stress are all excellent tools in learning how to keep your cool in a crisis.

Go with the Natural Flow of Things.

Go with the flow and learn to accept change rather than fighting against it or living with frustration and regrets. Understand that you are not separate from nature but are a part of it.

Make Simplicity the Foundation of your Lifestyle.

Live a simple life. The endless pursuit of money, possessions and power or falling into vices such as alcoholism, drugs, infidelity and gambling are ultimately detrimental to your health and wellbeing.

Continually audit your life and remove those things you don't need and that consume your time and resources.

Don't Allow Your Heart to be Clouded by Anger.

Anger negatively affects your health and clouds your judgement. Losing your temper over trivial things may cause you to drive away those you care about and bring hardship to yourself.

When faced with anger, learn to give yourself a moment, breathe deeply and face the situation calmly.

道場稽古 Dōjō Keiko (Group Training)

When looking to join a Dōjō, it is important to first gather as much information as possible and visit several different Dōjō before committing yourself.

There are many different styles of training and different cultures between individual Bujinkan Dōjō. Some emphasise basic forms, others self-defence, others historical applications. Although it is important to find a style of training that appeals to you, most important is that the instructor can teach the basics correctly, has a good foundation and has spent a considerable amount of time themselves training under a good teacher.

Ideally, you should attend group training sessions at a Dōjō three times a week, on an 'every other day' basis, such as Mondays, Wednesdays and Fridays. For those unable to train three times a week, you should still try to attend no less than one session a week, and if possible, a second one.

Despite initial enthusiasm, there are plenty of reasons you will find for not wanting to train (and most instructors have heard them all) but there are very few real excuses.

When you attend training sessions regularly over a few weeks, you will quickly get yourself into a rhythm in which going to the Dōjō becomes second nature to you.

Sometimes your training will need to be greatly modified due to injury or mobility issues. The nature and style of your training may also have to change in the long term as you age. The secret of longevity in Budō training is to listen to your body and adjust the intensity accordingly.

Frustration can occur in a group training environment when you are not able to perform the technique being demonstrated as competently as you would like. The important thing is to look for progress, not perfection. Each training session you attend is just another step along the path and real progress comes from slow and consistent practice.

一人稽古 Hitori Geiko (Solo-Training)

Hitori Keiko (solo-training) is just as important as regular training at the Dōjō.

Just ten to thirty minutes of basic technique training daily is sufficient to maintain good progress. Ideally, you should include a short solo-training session every morning or evening.

Practicing in small amounts daily has a cumulative effect that longer sessions done only once or twice a week do not.

Rather than aiming for hundreds of repetitions, limit yourself to just ten repetitions for each basic technique as this allows you to put your mind fully in the performance of each movement. When you practice with greater volume you risk ingraining bad habits into your muscle memory.

礼法 Reihō (Etiquette)

The basic etiquette of bowing, sitting and standing remains an important aspect of Budō training in Japan. Correct Reihō demonstrates proper mental preparedness, respect to the Dōjō, the teachings, the school and the teachers both past and present.

立礼 Ritsu-Rei (Standing Bow)

Ritsu-Rei is a bow performed from a standing posture. Respect is expressed to the Dōjō by bowing as you enter and leave the hall. Respect is shown towards your training partners by a bow before and after paired practice.

Figure 1-1-1 Ritsu-Rei

To perform Ritsu-Rei, stand in a natural posture with your feet slightly apart and your back straight. Your hands are held with the palms at your thighs. From this position bend the upper body forward to a position of approximately thirty degrees while keeping your back straight. Your fingertips should be just above your kneecaps. Hold this position for two to three seconds before returning to your original position.

正座 Seiza (Formal Sitting Position)

To sit in Seiza, start by standing in a natural posture with your feet slightly apart and your back straight. Your hands are held with the palms at your thighs. From this position, take a small step back with your left foot and kneel on your left knee while keeping the ball of your foot on the ground. Bring your right foot back to kneel on your right knee in the same manner. You should be sitting firmly on your heels with the balls of your feet on the floor. Raise your weight slightly off your heels and place your insteps on the ground with the feet side by side.

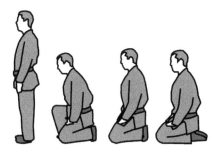

Figure 1-1-2 Seiza

Your buttocks should be resting on the top of your heels and your big toes placed together, but not on top of each other. There should be one fist space between your knees with the hands lightly resting on top of your thighs with the fingers closed.

To return to standing, raise your weight slightly off your heels and place the balls of your feet on the floor. From this position, step forward with your right foot, keeping both hands on the thighs. Stand up and bring the left foot forward so that it is in line with the right.

坐礼 Za-Rei (Seated Bow)

Za-Rei is a bow performed from Seiza. This bow is performed to the Kamiza (shrine or spiritual seat) as a part of the opening and closing ceremony and to each other at the start and finish of a training session.

Figure 1-1-3 Za-Rei

Sit in Seiza with your back straight and your hands on your thighs. Place both hands on the floor in front of your knees with your elbow out. From this position, bend the upper body forward until your head is approximately thirty centimetres from the floor while keeping your back straight. Hold this position for two to three seconds before returning to your original position.

神前礼 Shinzen-Rei (Bow to the Kamiza)

In the Bujinkan, each training session opens and closes with a traditional ceremony. This ceremony should be thought of as a vow or pledge for safe, enjoyable and meaningful training.

The Kamiza is the spiritual focal point of the Dōjō. For private Dōjō in Japan, the Kamiza will usually be in the form of a Kamidana (Spirit Shelf) which is set on a wall above eye level. The Kamidana will enshrine an object, usually a small mirror, and contain an Ofuda, a small charm obtained from a larger Shintō shrine. Offerings of rice, sake, water and other foods are left on the altar in addition to candles and flowers in accordance with the instructions for worship from the larger Shintō shrine.

In Japan, Dōjō rented in public gymnasiums and government buildings are not permitted to display religious items, so the Kamiza in these cases is usually just a direction nominated as the Shōmen (front) of the Dōjō.

A Kamiza does not need to be a shrine, but may simply be a piece of calligraphy, a photo of Hatsumi-sensei and Takamatsu-sensei or an object of significance to you. The physical form of the Kamiza is not as important as the feeling behind it; it functions as a focal point of your training and bowing to it expresses respect to the ancestors of the tradition.

To perform Shinzen-Rei, the instructor and students face the Kamiza of the Dōjō in Seiza with their hands held together in front of the chest, the palms touching each other.

The instructor recites the following short poem:

千早振る神の教えは常しえに正しき心身を守るらん
Chihayaburu, Kami no oshie wa tokoshie ni tadashiki kokoro mi o mamoruran.

The instructor then calls out:

詞韻波羅密大光明 Shikin Haramitsu Daikōmyō

The students then all repeat this loudly.

詞韻波羅密大光明 Shikin Haramitsu Daikōmyō

Everyone claps twice, bows, then claps once more and bows again.

The students and instructor then face each other and bow while saying:

Onegai Shimasu "Please (let's train)" to start training or
Arigatō Gozaimashita "Thank you" to finish training.

道場礼儀 Dōjō Reigi (Dōjō Etiquette)

Dōjō etiquette does involve some degree of formality that may appear foreign to many Western students, but Dōjō etiquette is not about cultural appropriation or pretending to be Japanese; it is an expression of respect to your teacher, the art and your fellow students as well as allowing training to be conducted in a safe and inclusive manner.

In Japan, training in the Bujinkan is typically informal, but informal social interaction between people in Japan is generally a little more polite than in Western culture.

The important thing is simply to show courtesy, consideration and respect without getting too uptight and formal:

- Always stop and bow before entering or leaving the Dōjō. In Japan, there will be an area by the door in which you remove your shoes before entering. Never step inside a Dōjō or on the mat without first removing your shoes.
- Cleaning in Budō is not considered janitorial but an important part of training. Help with cleaning after training and take any rubbish with you. It is important to leave the Dōjō as clean or cleaner than it was before you started training.
- Greet everyone when you arrive at the Dōjō and thank your training partners before departing.
- If you have an injury it is your responsibility to tell your training partners each time you train with them. It is also recommended that you mark the injury with tape on your uniform. Keep your finger and toenails clipped short and remove any jewellery. If a piece of jewellery cannot be removed it is recommended to tape over it.
- If you have a contagious disease (even if your think it is just a minor cold or flu) you should not go to training, nor should you ever attend if under the influence of alcohol or other drugs.
- If you are injured in training, you should let someone know and sit out the rest of the session or seek medical treatment immediately but always inform the instructor or a senior student first before leaving. If you are carrying an injury prior to training that you feel may be injured further by training, do not participate.

- Check the condition of any training equipment you are using each time and the area in which you are training for potential hazards. Be aware of what is going on around you at all times.
- Be attentive and listen carefully to instructions. Make sure you understand the activity before commencing to practice it; if you are uncertain, ask.
- Always apply yourself fully to each training session. Use your common sense and try to be courteous, respectful and helpful to all members of your Dōjō. A Dōjō is not a gym and students are not customers, think about how you can contribute in helping everyone to get the most out of each training session.

道場訓 Dōjō Kun (Laws of the Dōjō)

1. Know that Nintai (endurance / patience) can be found if you take a moment's pause.
2. Know that the path of man is that of justice.
3. Renounce the heart of greed, laziness and favouritism.
4. Think of sadness and resentment as natural states. Obtain the enlightenment of Fudōshin (the immovable heart).
5. Don't let your heart stray from the path of loyalty and filial piety. Aspire to a deep study of the ways of the literary and martial arts.

Following the 5 rules above is the law of the Dōjō.

Written:

Meiji 23 (1890) Spring, Toda Shinryuken Masamitsu

Shôwa 33 (1958) March, Takamatsu Toshitsugu (Uou)

Hatsumi Masaaki (Byakuryu)

PHYSICAL PREPARATION

柔軟体操と歩行法

龍体運動 Ryūtai Undō (Dragon Body Stretching Exercises)

The Ryūtai Undō are made up of four basic exercises practiced from a seated position on the floor. These exercises have been adapted from a popular Japanese health system called Makkō-hō.

Makkō-hō was founded by Wataru Nagai in 1933 and is practiced by tens of thousands of people all over Japan. Wataru Nagai developed the system after suffering a stroke at the age of forty-two and becoming paralysed down one side of his body. Through the initial practice of bowing from standing and sitting to a Buddhist shrine as a show of devotion, he came upon this system as a means of correcting the alignment of the pelvis and spinal column - which in turn rejuvenates the circulation and nervous system.

We refer to our version of this system as Ryūtai Undō (Dragon Body Stretching), although it contains only small variations from the original Makkō-hō exercises.

Each of the basic exercises stretches the legs and hips in a different position to target the iliotibial (IT) band tendon that runs down the length of the outer thigh, the hamstrings that run down the backs of the leg, the inner thighs (adductors) and the quadriceps that run down the front of the thigh. From a stretched position, you perform a bowing motion in time with your breathing and maintain a straight back while pivoting from the sacrum at the base of the spine in order to gently realign your pelvis back to its natural position.

Ryūtai Undō Exercise 1

In a seated position on the floor, bring your heels together while keeping your back perfectly straight. The soles of your feet should be turned up as much as possible and your heels should be in line with your knees. Ideally, your knees should rest on the floor. If they do not, then you may press lightly on your knees with your hands, but do not try to force them down. Keep your eyes directly forward, your back straight and your chest out as looking down will cause your head to roll forward and your spine to bend. Keeping your back straight, place your hands in front of you and bend at the waist to bring your chest flat on the floor in front of you in time with your exhalation.

Figure 1-2-1 Ryūtai Undō Exercise 1

This exercise is practiced dynamically by raising and lowering your body from the first to final position very slowly and in time with your natural breathing for eight repetitions.

In the beginning, it is only necessary to lean your upper body forward until you feel a stretch. Try to increase your forward bend by just one centimetre each day until you are able to get your chest all the way to the floor. Maintain a steady breathing pattern throughout.

Ryūtai Undō Exercise 2

While in a seated position on the floor, extend both of your legs forward and keep your back perfectly straight. Pull your toes back towards you so as your feet are held at an angle of sixty degrees to your legs. Keep your eyes looking directly forward and your chest out.

Once you have succeeded in keeping your back straight, while maintaining the same posture, twist your upper body to face your left side and hold for eight breaths. Next, twist the upper body to face your right side and hold for another eight breaths.

Then return to the first position of the exercise. Finally, while keeping your back straight, bend forward at your waist until your chest is lying flat on your legs.

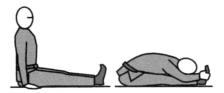

Figure 1-2-2 Ryūtai Undō Exercise 2

This exercise is practiced dynamically by raising and lowering your body from the first to final position very slowly and in time with your natural breathing for eight repetitions.

In the beginning, it is only necessary to lean your upper body forward until you feel a stretch. The purpose of this exercise is not to bring the head to the knees but to bend forward from the waist while maintaining a straight back. Try to increase your forward bend by just one centimetre each day until you are able to go through the full range of motion. Maintain a steady breathing pattern throughout.

Ryūtai Undō Exercise 3

While in a seated position on the floor, open your legs as far apart as possible and keep your back perfectly straight. Pull your toes back towards you so that your feet are held at an angle of sixty degrees to your legs. Keep your eyes looking directly forward and your chest out.

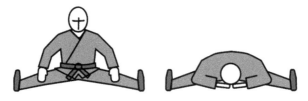

Figure 1-2-3 Ryūtai Undō Exercise 3

Once you have succeeded in keeping your back straight, maintaining the same posture, place your hands in front of you and lean your upper body forward by bending at the waist until your stomach lies flat on the floor.

This exercise is practiced dynamically by raising and lowering your body from the first to final position very slowly and in time with your natural breathing for eight repetitions.

In the beginning, it is only necessary to lean your upper body forward until you feel a stretch. Try to increase your forward bend by just one centimetre each day until you are able to bring your stomach flat on the floor. Maintain a steady breathing pattern throughout.

You can make this exercise more challenging by grasping the big toes of each foot with your hands while doing this exercise.

Figure 1-2-4 Variation of Ryūtai Undō Exercise 3

Ryūtai Undō Exercise 4

Kneel in a position similar to Seiza, but with your buttocks seated on the floor between your feet. Your back should be kept perfectly straight with your eyes looking directly forward and your chest out. Your shin bones should be in contact with the floor from your knees to the tips of your toes. Hold this position for eight breaths.

If your buttocks do not reach the floor, then you should place a cushion or folded towel of a suitable height underneath to sit on and provide support.

Next, while keeping your shins on the floor, stand up on your knees and push your thighs forward as you bend your back to grasp your heels with the palms of your hands. Beginners can take one heel at a time by tilting the shoulders individually. While pressing down on the soles of your feet, lift your hips, tighten your buttocks and take your head as far back as possible. Hold this position for eight breaths then return to the first position of the exercise.

Figure 1-2-5 Ryūtai Undō Exercise 4

The next part of the exercise involves you leaning back to touch the floor with your back and shoulders. Firstly, while keeping your shins on the floor, lean backward and lower yourself to your elbows. Then, if you are able, lie so that your back is flat on the floor with your arms stretched out above your head. While holding this position, rotate the palms of your hands inside and out for thirty repetitions in time with your breathing.

In the beginning, and until you are flexible enough to safely take the final position, you may stack cushions behind you or use a yoga bolster to lie back on. If you are practising with another person, you can have them support you in the exercise.

Figure 1-2-6 Ryūtai Undō Exercise 4 Modified Position

In addition to the basic exercise, you may also lie on the floor and place your heels by your buttocks and your palms on the floor at either side of your head. From here you can push your torso up in one movement and hold for eight breaths.

Figure 1-2-7 Ryūtai Undō Exercise 4 Additional Position

呼吸法 Kokyū-hō (Breathing Exercises)

The Kokyū-hō are made up of three basic deep breathing exercises that are practiced from a seated position in the floor. Deep breathing exercises help detoxify the body, improve the blood flow, stimulate the lymphatic system and reduce stress. For the martial artist, deep breathing exercises also assist in improving posture, core strength and breath control.

深呼吸三阿吽 Shinkokyū San Aum ("Three Aum" Deep Breathing)

Exercise 1

Kneel in Seiza. Your back should be kept perfectly straight, your eyes looking directly forward and your chest out. Breathe in deeply while opening your shoulders and lifting your chest up, then breathe out as you lean slightly forward and drop your shoulders to completely exhale all the air from your lungs. Repeat eight times.

Figure 1-2-8 Frontal Breathing

Exercise 2

From Seiza, twist to face your right side as you pull back your right shoulder and inhale deeply. While holding the breath, drop your right shoulder and crunch down while still facing to your right side then turn back to the front while completely exhaling all the air from your lungs. Do the same exercise on the left side. Repeat eight times.

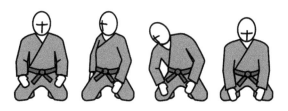

Figure 1-2-9 Left-Right Deep Breathing

Exercise 3

While seated on the floor, extend both of your legs forward, without bending them, and keep your back perfectly straight. Keep your eyes looking directly forward and your chest out. Extend your hands out straight to either side. Bend forward at the waist and extend your hands forward to touch your toes while completely exhaling all the air from your lungs. Breathe in deeply as you return to the original position with your hands extended out to either side. Repeat eight times.

Figure 1-2-10 Extension Deep Breathing

How to Practice Ryūtai Undō and Kokyū-hō

These exercises should be performed every day. When practising, do not be in a rush as trying to make too much progress too quickly will only lead to injury. Even with daily practice, it may take two years or more to reach your full range of motion.

1. Before you begin, sit down on the floor and relax your body for a few minutes, concentrate on keeping your spine straight and allow yourself to breath naturally.
2. Next, take one of your feet and rotate the big toe several times in each direction, followed by your other toes individually. Then grasp your whole foot and rotate the ankle joint several times both clockwise and anticlockwise. Massage the sole of your foot by applying firm pressure with your thumbs. Then repeat for the other foot.
3. Practice Ryūtai Undō Exercises 1 to 3 for eight repetitions in time with your breathing, then repeat the Ryūtai Undō Exercises 1 to 3

again for a second set of eight repetitions. If time permits then add a third set of eight repetitions.

4. Practice Ryūtai Undō Exercise 4
5. Next, stand up and swing your right leg up as high as you can while maintaining a straight leg for two repetitions then repeat for the left leg.
6. Swing your right leg up sideways as high as you can while maintaining a straight leg for two repetitions. You may bend forward slightly at the waist to increase the height of the leg swing. Repeat for the left leg.
7. Finally, swing your right leg up backwards as high as you can while maintaining a straight leg for two repetitions. Repeat for the left leg.
8. Sit back down on the floor in Seiza and practice Kokyū-hō exercises 1 to 3
9. Bring your knees up to your chest, then relax and roll up and down your back on the floor to gently massage your spine.
10. Finally, sit or lie down on the floor and relax your body for a few minutes, allowing yourself to breath naturally.

Figure 1-2-11 Ashi-Furi

Figure 1-2-12 Massaging the Spine

歩行法 Hokō-hō (Walking Method)

In old Japan, the legs were referred to as the "second heart", because walking and moving the legs is also a way of pumping more blood through your body. Daily walking benefits your health in many ways, including improving your fitness, aiding recovery from training sessions, relieving stress and improving your quality of sleep.

Walking is also a form of meditation. You can work on your awareness by maintaining a 'tenfold gaze', which means not allowing your consciousness to fix on a single point externally or internally (in your mind) but to open up your awareness to all points around you simultaneously.

Most importantly, walking is the fundamental tool for training yourself in the correct footwork for Budō Taijutsu and should be practiced for one to three hours daily.

As you walk you should appear to float along as if on a cushion of air, or like a small boat floating along a calm lake. Called Ukimi no Jutsu (Floating Body Technique), this is achieved by taking lighter steps and ensuring that your ankles, knees and hips travel along a level path.

As you walk, use your whole foot by rolling your weight from your heel, across your arch, then from your little toe to your big toe. Your foot is made up of many muscles, joints, bones and ligaments, all of which can move.

Keep your back straight, chest out and look forward. There is no need to look at your feet, your brain will remember what it has seen in front of it before you get there.

Use the muscles of your legs and core to support yourself as you walk. Your joints will tire quickly if you stride out and lock your knees with each step; by using your musculature to support yourself, you can distribute the work over your whole body.

By taking smaller steps and maintaining a very small bend in your knees you can keep your weight off your joints significantly. Smaller, lighter and faster steps are more efficient than big strides.

Avoid swaying from side to side, bobbing up and down, stiffening your legs or dragging your feet.

If you have dogs, walking with them is excellent training for your footwork, because dogs will naturally stop and start, walking at an erratic pace.

Try to move naturally with the animals – when they go quicker, jog with them, if they stop suddenly to sniff something, stop with them. This method of training through dog walking is also an efficient way for learning to keep your stability through good footwork so that you are always in control of the leash and never pulled off balance or knocked over.

歩行法の稽古 Hokō-hō no Keiko (Walking Training Methods)

In addition to your basic daily walking practice, there are several other more specialised training methods for walking that you may wish to try.

氷上歩行 Hyōjō Hokō (Walking on ice)

Hyōjō Hokō is the practice of walking and training on ice while wearing Geta (Japanese wooden clogs) as an extreme method of learning to maintain your balance. As you traverse the slippery surface, keep your centre of gravity low and your steps small while keeping your weight centred over your feet.

Before employing this training, it is important to have a good foundation in Ukemi (breakfalling and rolling) as you will certainly slip and fall many times.

石歩き Ishi Aruki (Walking on rocks)

This training method is to teach how to distribute your weight over your feet correctly and was also used in both old Japan and China as a way of stimulating the feet, body and vital organs.

Start off by standing or walking barefoot on large, smooth river rocks and study how your feet must adjust in order to grip the rocks and control your balance.

After you have mastered walking barefoot over large smooth rocks comfortably, you can then start practicing walking on smaller rocks and pebbles. Study how you can move across them lightly without causing pain to the soles of your feet by placing and shifting your body weight over your feet so as you distribute your mass more equally.

一本歯下駄 Ippon-ha Geta (Single Tooth Clogs)

Ippon-ha Geta (single tooth clogs) - also known as Tengu Geta (Goblin Clogs) are used as a training tool to ensure correct footwork and posture. In order to walk in Ippon-ha Geta without falling over, your balance needs to be centred correctly over your feet.

They were originally worn by Yamabushi (Buddhist monks who practiced asceticism in the mountains) as they climbed steep mountain paths.

Figure 1-2-13 Ippon-ha Geta

トカゲ歩き Tokage Aruki (Lizard Walking)

This is a crawling method in which you only support yourself on your hands and the balls of your feet as you move forwards or backwards.

Try and keep your body low to the floor so as the end of your belt is touching the mat at all times. Keep your body level as you move forwards rather than bouncing up and down.

Figure 1-2-14 Tokage Aruki

鷹の舞 Taka no Mai (The Dance of the Hawk)

Taka no Mai is a basic exercise to teach the correct body alignment and weight shifting for power generation. This exercise also assists in developing good flexibility, leg and core strength. Hold each posture for a few breaths and move from one to the next along the same plane, without bobbing up and down.

1. Uchū-Gasshō: Stand with your hands in front of your chest and your fingers folded together.
2. Hira Ichimonji no Kamae: Step out so as the insides of your heels are in line with the outsides of your shoulders. Your feet should be turned out slightly with your knees in line with your feet. Extend your arms straight out to either side.
3. Ihen no Kamae: While keeping your hips level, turn your left foot to your left and shift your body weight across to it. Keep your feet the same width apart and your shoulders and hips level. Allow your left knee to travel only just beyond the front of your toes.
4. Return to Hira Ichimonji no Kamae.
5. Ihen no Kamae: While keeping your hips level, turn your right foot to your right and shift your body weight across to it. Keep your feet the same width apart and your shoulders and hips level. Allow your right knee to travel only just beyond the front of your toes.
6. Return to Hira Ichimonji no Kamae.
7. Return to the Uchū-Gasshō.

Figure 1-2-15 Taka no Mai

3

SHISEI AND KAMAE (POSTURE AND BODY STRUCTURE)

姿勢と構え

姿勢 Shisei (Posture)

Shisei is the foundation of good technique. Correct posture allows the movement of your body to be lighter, smoother and more agile.

When standing, you are connected to the earth through the soles of your feet. Gravity acts on your bodyweight through your body's centreline (the Chūshin-Sen). If your body stands in its natural alignment, gravity will act on it in such a way as to require almost no addition muscular tension to hold it in position.

Your head should sit level. If your head rolls forward it also pulls your body's centre of gravity forward, thus placing tension through the muscles of your back and legs. Similarly, if you allow your head to roll backwards, it puts tension into the muscles of the front of your body.

Koshi, Hara and Tanden are general terms in the Japanese martial arts for the important postural muscles, located around your pelvis, lower back and abdomen. Once your pelvis is correctly aligned, all the vertebrae of your spine will naturally align themselves to their correct position and a good posture will be easily maintained.

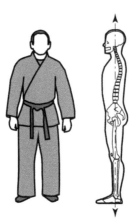

Figure 1.3.1: Shisei

Developing these postural muscles (core strength) and maintaining flexibility around your hip joints will greatly improve your body's natural stability.

The first task is to develop and maintain the mobility around your hips and legs to the point where they regain their full range of motion and your pelvis sits in its correct alignment. Next is to develop and strengthen your internal postural muscles,

Maintaining good posture may feel easy when standing still, but you need to maintain this alignment throughout your Taijutsu practice. Postural alignment is easy to lose when you look down at your feet, thrust your hips back to get lower or move your head or upper body independently.

As you practice, you will constantly catch yourself out of good postural alignment, it is then a matter of correcting yourself on the spot again and again until correct posture becomes second nature to you.

構え Kamae (Body Structure / Base)

More than just fixed positions of attack and defence, Kamae exist as points within sequences of movement. The basic forms of Kamae teach the efficient and balanced configuration of the body and correct distancing.

You should maintain a body structure that is simultaneously manoeuvrable and stable. Stability allows you to keep yourself in balance and deliver attacks from a strong base. Manoeuvrability allows you to avoid your opponent's attacks and to close in quickly to counterattack.

The first step is to stand in each Kamae and allow your body to feel and remember each position.

There is often debate about how deep Kamae should be taken. The answer is to find the 'balance of effort and ease' in that if your posture is too high, you lose the connection between your upper and lower body, but by going too low you lose your manoeuvrability. Find that point in-between, in which your body has both structure *and* freedom of movement, but keep in mind that this point is not fixed; as your strength and flexibility improves, your Kamae may need to deepen to accommodate.

The Kamae vary between the different Ryūha (schools), but in this chapter, we will examine four basic Kamae from the Kihon Gata (Basic Forms) which have their origin in Gyokko Ryū Kosshijutsu.

•Shizentai

•Ichimonji no Kamae

•Hichō no Kamae

•Jūmonji no Kamae

自然体 Shizentai (Natural Posture)

Shizentai is the starting point, as it is a posture that allows you to respond or move in any direction. The posture Shizentai keeps your hands free, allowing them to strike, grab or draw a weapon.

Stand up straight, keep your shoulders back, chest out and head up. Your shoulders and neck should be free of tension. Don't lock your knees but allow them to bend very slightly so as the weight of your body is supported by your leg muscles and not your joints.

Figure 1.3.2: Shizentai

一文字の構え Ichimonji no Kamae

From a natural posture, step back with your right foot and lower your hips with the feeling of sitting into the Kamae. Your left foot should be facing directly forward in line with your left knee and your right foot turned out and in line with your right knee. The insides of your heels should be in line with the outsides of your shoulders.

Figure 1.3.3: Ichimonji no Kamae

Keep your back straight and don't allow your hips to stick out behind you. Extend your left arm forward, but very slightly bent, with your left hand open and pointed at the centre of your opponent. Your right hand may be placed either at the elbow joint of your left arm or up by your right ear in a relaxed fist with your thumb pointed upwards. Relax your shoulders, neck, face and jaw. Keep your head up and looking forward.

飛鳥の構え Hichō no Kamae

Turn your right foot ninety degrees to your opponent and shift your weight back onto your right leg so as you are centred over the foot. Bring your left foot up to your right knee, with your left knee pointed in the direction of your opponent. Keep your back straight by pushing up from below. Extend your left arm forward, but very slightly bent, with your left hand open and pointed at the centre of the opponent. Your right hand may be placed either at the elbow joint of your left arm or high above your head in a relaxed fist with your thumb pointed upwards. Relax your shoulders, neck, face and jaw. Keep your head up and looking forward.

Figure 1.3.4: Hichō no Kamae

The ability to shift your weight so that it is centred over one foot while remaining stable is an important basic skill, fundamental to many of the techniques of Budō Taijutsu. The name Hichō means "flying bird". As your body weight is stable and supported over your right foot, your left foot can touch down anywhere around its radius, like a bird.

Many people find it very difficult to balance in this posture because they try to stabilise themselves by swaying their hips or body from the centre. Instead, try and have the feeling of pushing down through the floor with your supporting leg while pushing up to the ceiling with your head. Once you can stand in this Kamae for a minute each side, try doing the same with your eyes closed.

十文字の構え Jūmonji no Kamae

Bring your right foot back half a step and lower your hips into the Kamae. Your right and left feet should be turned slightly out with your knees in line with them. From this position, you should be able to strike or grab with either hand equally well. The insides of your heels should be in line with the outsides of your shoulders. Your left arm is placed in front of your right in the form of a cross, held at your chest level, with each of your hands in a relaxed fist with the thumbs pointing upwards. Relax your shoulders, neck, face and jaw. Keep your head up and looking forward.

Figure 1.3.5: Jūmonji no Kamae

4

ATEKOMI (STRIKING)

當込

Atekomi (more conventionally known as 'Atemi' in the Japanese martial arts) are techniques that use any part of the body to strike at the opponent.

Atekomi can be used to stun, unbalance, subdue, incapacitate or even deliver a fatal blow to an adversary.

拳体一如 Ken Tai Ichi-Jo (The Strike and Body as One)

The important principle of Atekomi is to remove the tension from the upper body and use the power of the legs and torso behind each strike. Rather than compete for speed and power, strikes should be correctly delivered at Kyūsho (vital points) with good alignment and technique.

Strikes are more effective when delivered from close range than far away, as they are harder for the opponent to see and respond against. Correct Atekomi should strike through and damage the core of the opponent rather than striking at the surface.

Atekomi techniques were historically trained by striking a post that had been padded with straw and then was bound by tightly wrapping it in cloth or leather to the thickness of a human body. Heavy bags, focus mitts and kick shields can be used for the same purpose.

不動拳 Fudō-Ken

Fudō-Ken is a conventional 'clenched fist'. The strike is delivered with the two knuckles of your index and middle fingers. There is no need to rotate your fist as you punch, as it can be simply thrust at your opponent in its natural vertical alignment.

Figure 1.4.1: Fudō-Ken

Do not clench your fist hard; rather, keep it as relaxed as if you were holding a quail egg in your hand: too loose and the egg will fall, too tight and the egg will break. It is only necessary to clench your fist tighter on impact.

Figure 1.4.2: Fudō-Ken Tsuki

The power of the strike is transmitted through the drive of your elbow forward, which in turn, stretches your back muscles (the trapezius) right across your back to your pelvis – connecting your upper and lower body structures.

The alignment of your knuckles is very important. The strike should result in a straight line from your knuckles through your wrist and forearm to your elbow.

Taking the time to practice the correct alignment of your fist to your elbow is important for the sake of injury prevention. You could damage the bones of your wrist if it bends forwards or backwards as you punch.

指環拳 Shikan-Ken

To form this fist, you bend the middle knuckles of your hand and press your thumb against your index finger.

As with Fudō-Ken, Shikan-Ken is usually thrust at your opponent vertically, although it may be rotated to strike specific targets such as the neck.

Figure 1.4.3: Shikan-Ken

Shikan-Ken provides a slightly greater reach and a more penetrating strike than a conventional clenched fist.

With Shikan-Ken, it is even more important to ensure that the alignment of your hand and arm are correct and that the fist is driven from your elbow.

Pressing your thumb to the knuckle of your index finger holds the structure of the fist together; the rest of your hand should stay soft and relaxed.

蝦蛄拳 Shako-Ken

Shako-Ken is a strike made with the palm and five fingertips of the hand. After the strike is delivered with the palm, you can then push your fingers forward to gouge or grab. As with all punches, the power is transmitted from the drive of your elbow forward.

Figure 1.4.4: Shako-Ken

This strike is very effective against the jaw and face and can also be used as a grabbing strike against targets on the body.

指刀拳 Shitō-Ken

(Also known as 拇指拳 Boshi-Ken)

To form this fist, you extend the tip of your thumb beyond your index finger and press them together. Your other fingers should remain relaxed. This strike is particularly effective against the ribs or neck of the opponent.

Figure 1.4.5: Shitō-Ken

Figure 1.4.6: Shitō-Ken Tsuki

A small object such as a pen or key can also be held between your thumb and index finger to use it as a concealed weapon.

手刀拳 Shutō-Ken

(Also known as 起転拳 Kiten-Ken)

Shutō-Ken is a strike using the edge of the hand from the bottom knuckle of the little finger to the wrist. This strike is initiated from a closed fist, with the fingers half-opened on impact.

Figure 1.4.7: Shutō-Ken

表手刀 Omote-Shutō

Omote-Shutō is delivered palm up and the action should be like that of throwing a ball, in which fingers are half-opened at the point of impact corresponding to the point in which the ball is released.

Figure 1.4.8: Omote Shutō

裏手刀 Ura-Shutō

Ura-Shutō is delivered palm down with a similar feeling of the hand being cast forward and the fingers half-opened upon impact.

Figure 1.4.9: Ura-Shutō

三心突き Sanshin-Tsuki

Sanshin-Tsuki is a strike delivered with the index, middle and ring fingers supported by the thumb. The fingers should be squeezed together upon impact.

This strike utilises the swing of the arm as it scoops up from below with an action similar to that of bowling a ball underarm. This strike is particularly effective when swung up at the ribs of the opponent.

Figure 1.4.10: Sanshin-Tsuki

Figure 1.4.11: Sanshin-Tsuki Delivery

八葉拳 Happa-Ken

Happa-Ken is a strike performed by slapping the palms of both hands simultaneously at the opponent's ears. This is a deceptively dangerous strike, which can cause serious damage to a person's eardrums.

Figure 1.4.12: Happa-Ken

前方蹴り Zenpō-Keri (Front Kick)

Swing your leg up until your knee almost touches your chest, then pull your toes back as you thrust forward with your heel at the target. Your supporting leg should be slightly bent and your centre of gravity stable.

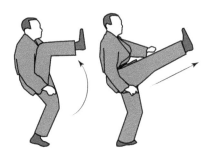

Figure 1.4.13: Zenpō-Keri

横蹴り Yoko-Keri (Side Kick)

Swing your leg up until your knee almost touches the outside of your shoulder, then pull your toes back as you thrust with your heel at the target. Your supporting leg should be slightly bent and your centre of gravity stable. Ensure your kicking foot is kept vertical.

Figure 1.4.14: Yoko-Keri

後蹴り Ushiro-Keri (Back Kick)

Bend forward at the waist (you may touch the floor with your hands if necessary) as you pull your toes back and allow your heel to thrust backward at the target. Your right foot should brush the inside of the knee of your supporting as you kick.

Figure 1.4.15: Ushiro Keri

掬い蹴り **Sukui-Geri (Scooping Kick)**

Kick up with the inside edge of your foot. This kick is mostly utilised to target the groin but can also be used to kick up at the opponent's jaw.

Figure 1.4.16: Sukui Geri

鉤蹴り(内側) **Kagi-Geri Uchi-Gawa (Hook Kick - Inside)**

Rotate your foot horizontally to kick to the inside of the opponent's knee joint with your heel. The sole of your foot should be rotated upward as much as possible. This kick can also be used to target the inside thigh or lower leg.

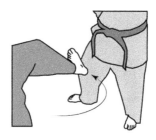

Figure 1.4.17 Kagi-Geri Uchi-Gawa

鉤蹴り (外側) Kagi-Geri Soto-Gawa (Hook Kick - Outside)

Rotate your foot horizontally to kick to the outside of the opponent's knee joint with your heel. The sole of your foot should be rotated upward as much as possible. This kick can also be used to target the outer thigh or lower leg.

Figure 1.4.18: Kagi-Geri Soto-Gawa

宝拳十六法 **Hōken Juroppō (The Sixteen Treasure Fists)**

The Hōken Juroppō are a list classifying sixteen areas of the body used for Atekomi techniques within Budō Taijutsu. Each of these 'fists' can be employed in many different ways and from many different directions.

After mastering each one individually, you can study using them in combination.

Examples include changing from Shutō-ken to Shitō-Ken; Fudō-Ken to Shuki-Ken to Shutō-Ken; Sokuyaku-Ken to Sokugyaku-Ken; Happa-Ken to Kikaku-Ken.

1. 鬼角拳 **Kikaku-Ken**: The forehead, rear or sides of the head.
2. 手起拳 **Shuki-Ken**: The elbow
3. 不動拳 **Fudō-Ken**: The clenched fist.
4. 手刀拳・起転拳 **Shutō-Ken/Kiten-Ken**: Edge of the hand.
5. 指針拳 **Shishin-Ken**: The little finger used to gouge or hook.
6. 指端拳 **Shitan-Ken**: The fingertips used to strike in various forms.
7. 蝦蛄拳 **Shako-Ken**: The palm and five fingers used together.
8. 指刀拳 **Shitō-Ken**: *(Also known as Boshi-Ken)* The thumb.
9. 指環拳 **Shikan-Ken**: The extended knuckles.
10. 骨法拳 **Koppō-Ken**: The thumb joint supported by the fist.
11. 八葉拳 **Happa-Ken**: Both palms struck simultaneously at the ears.
12. 足躍拳 **Sokuyaku-Ken**: The heel and sole of the foot.
13. 足起拳 **Sokki-Ken**: The knee.
14. 足逆拳 **Sokugyaku-Ken**: The toes.
15. 体拳 **Tai-Ken**: The whole body as one unit.
16. 気拳 **Ki-Ken**: A strike made with the power of the spirit.

5

KYŪSHO (VITAL POINTS)
急所

Kyūsho (the vital points of the human body), under the application of light pressure administered by a qualified therapist, can assist with healing and improved mobility.

These same points, under the application of force in combat, can bring about pain, physical damage, unconsciousness and even death.

While there are differences in the names and locations of Kyūsho between the different schools, I have presented a general list of the points depicted in the descriptions of the basic Kata and those often referred to in general training.

This list has been compiled for reference only. I have not pinpointed the exact locations or detailed the effects as this needs to be taught by a competent teacher.

It should also be noted that the exact location and effect of the different Kyūsho varies between individuals.

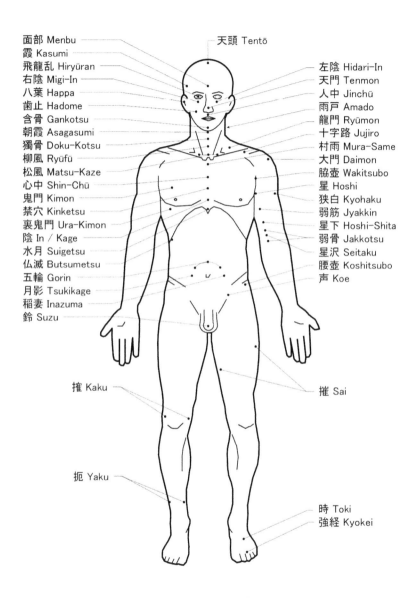

面部 Menbu
霞 Kasumi
飛龍乱 Hiryūran
右陰 Migi-In
八葉 Happa
歯止 Hadome
含骨 Gankotsu
朝霞 Asagasumi
獨骨 Doku-Kotsu
柳風 Ryūfū
松風 Matsu-Kaze
心中 Shin-Chū
鬼門 Kimon
禁穴 Kinketsu
裏鬼門 Ura-Kimon
陰 In / Kage
水月 Suigetsu
仏滅 Butsumetsu
五輪 Gorin
月影 Tsukikage
稲妻 Inazuma
鈴 Suzu

天頭 Tentō

左陰 Hidari-In
天門 Tenmon
人中 Jinchū
雨戸 Amado
龍門 Ryūmon
十字路 Jujiro
村雨 Mura-Same
大門 Daimon
脇壺 Wakitsubo
星 Hoshi
狭白 Kyohaku
弱筋 Jyakkin
星下 Hoshi-Shita
弱骨 Jakkotsu
星沢 Seitaku
腰壺 Koshitsubo
声 Koe

摧 Kaku

摧 Sai

扼 Yaku

時 Toki
強経 Kyokei

Figure 1.5.1: Kyūsho Front

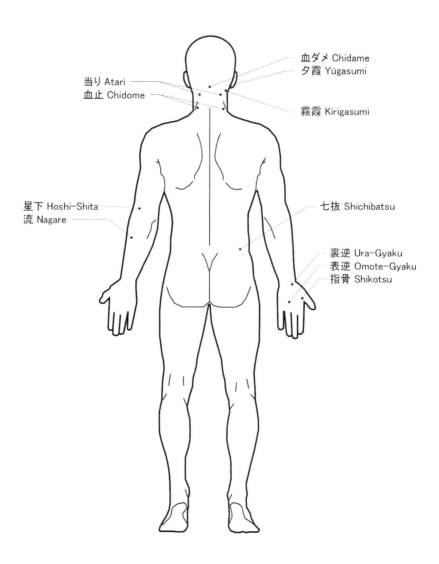

当り Atari
血止 Chidome

星下 Hoshi-Shita
流 Nagare

血ダメ Chidame
夕霞 Yūgasumi

霧霞 Kirigasumi

七抜 Shichibatsu

裏逆 Ura-Gyaku
表逆 Omote-Gyaku
指骨 Shikotsu

Figure 1.5.2: Kyūsho Back

頭 **Atama (Head)**

- 天頭 Tentō: The indentation at the top of the head.
- 面部 Menbu: The face / forehead.
- 霞 Kasumi: The temple.
- 飛龍乱 Hiryūran: The eyeball.
- 八葉 Happa: Both ears when slapped simultaneously with the palms of the hands.
- 右陰 Migi-In: The cheekbone below the right eye.
- 左陰 Hidari-In: The cheekbone below the left eye.
- 天門 Tenmon: The nose.
- 人中 Jinchū: Under the nose.
- 歯止 Hadome: The point where the teeth connect to the upper jaw between the nose and cheekbone.
- 含骨 Gankotsu: The point of the chin.
- 朝霞 Asagasumi: Under the jaw at the point of the chin.
- 夕霞 Yūgasumi: The indentation behind the earlobe.
- 霧霞 Kirigasumi: The edge of the jaw below the ear.
- 当り Atari: The boney protrusion at the back of the head, behind the ear.
- 血止 Chidome: The sides of the neck at the back of the head.
- 血ダメ Chidame: The indentation at the back of the head.

胴 **Dō (Torso)**

- 仏滅 Butsumetsu: The floating ribs.
- 心中 Shin-Chū: Mid-point of the chest.
- 鬼門 Kimon: Point above the pectoral muscle.
- 裏鬼門 Ura-Kimon: The ribs below the pectoral muscle.
- 禁穴 Kinketsu: The breast bone (sternum).
- 陰 In / Kage: The bottom of the breast bone above the solar plexus.
- 水月 Suigetsu: The solar plexus (Also known as 獅子乱 Shishiran).
- 五輪 Gorin: Five points surrounding the navel.
- 月影 Tsukikage: Point to the right of the navel.
- 稲妻 Inazuma: Point to the left of the navel.

- 七抜 Shichibatsu: Point of the hip inside the ridge of the pelvis (illiac crest).

首 Kubi (Neck)

- 雨戸 Amado: Side of the neck.
- 龍門 Ryūmon: The indentation above the collar bone.
- 十字路 Jujiro: The joint of the collar bone to the front of the shoulder.
- 村雨 Mura-Same: The top of the breastbone.
- 柳風 Ryūfū: The windpipe.
- 獨骨 Doku-Kotsu: The Adam's apple.
- 松風 Matsu-Kaze: The indentations at the base of the neck made up of: *Toki no Atari*: The jugular notch, *Ichiji*: To the left of the windpipe, *Santō*: To the right of the windpipe.

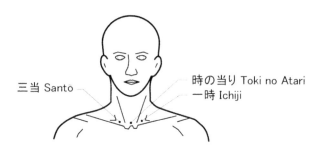

Figure 1.5.3: Matsu-Kaze

腕 Ude (Arms)

- 脇壺 Wakitsubo: Under the armpit.
- 星 Hoshi: Inside of the upper arm, just below the armpit.
- 弱筋 Jyakkin: Points located on the inside of the upper arm.
- 星下 Hoshi-Shita: Point on the inside of the upper arm just above the elbow joint.

- 弱骨 Jakkotsu: The areas above and below the elbow joint.
- 星沢 Seitaku: Indentation at the inside of the elbow joint.
- 狭白 Kyohaku: The upper arm below the shoulder muscle.
- 大門 Daimon: The top of the shoulder joint.
- 流 Nagare: Point on the outside of the forearm.
- 表逆 Omote-Gyaku: Back of the hand.
- 裏逆 Ura-Gyaku: Point just above the wrist at the base of the thumb.
- 指骨 Shikotsu: The indentation at the joint between the thumb and index finger.

足 Ashi (Legs)

- 鈴 Suzu: The testicles (Also known as 虎勢 Kosei).
- 声 Koe: Indentation at the groin crease.
- 腰壺 Koshitsubo: Point at the middle of the hip joint.
- 摧 Sai: Inside or outside of the thigh (Also known as 谷 Tani).
- 摧 Kaku: Inside or outside of the knee joint.
- 扼 Yaku: Inside or outside of the lower leg.
- 時 Toki: Point at the top of the foot.
- 強経 Kyokei: Top of the five toes.

6

TAI-SABAKI (EVASION)

体捌き

体捌き Tai-Sabaki (Evasion)

Tai-Sabaki is utilised to evade your opponent's attack, while simultaneously opening up target areas on his body to counterattack.

It is always preferable to use Tai-Sabaki to evade, rather than blocking a strike with your arms while your body remains stationary.

Tai-Sabaki should be practiced in the following ten directions:

- Forward and backward.
- Left and right.
- Diagonally backward to the left and right.
- Diagonally forward to the left and right.
- Jumping up and dropping down low.

When evading an attack, it is important to maintain your balance and body structure at all times. Keep the following basic principles in mind when studying Tai-Sabaki:

Keep your hips and shoulders level.

If your shoulder drops and / or hips lift or twist, then you will be putting excess tension into your body and making yourself easier to unbalance. A balanced body structure requires that your hips and shoulders are level at all times.

Keep your feet the same width apart.

As you take a step, allow your other foot to slide with it to maintain a constant distance between them.

Keep your footwork light.

Your movement should appear light and relaxed while being simultaneously strongly grounded, centred and stable.

As with your basic walking technique, utilise Ukimi no Jutsu (Floating Body Technique). Your body should not sway or rise up and down with each step. In Japan, this is described as moving like a small boat across a calm lake - or like a legless apparition, floating across the floor.

Understand distance.

Bujinkan Dōjō Budō Taijutsu is often referred to as "The Martial Art of Distance". Fundamental to the art is the intuitive understanding of distance, how to manipulate your opponent's perception of distance and how to control the space between yourself and your opponent.

The difference between being in a perfect position to being too close or too far away from your opponent is very small. The perfect position will be different for every situation and every opponent.

Distance in Budō Taijutsu is not only concerning points in three-dimensional space but also time (the fourth dimension). The physical distance between objects affects the time to travel between them. Through years of accumulated practice, your body will gain an intuitive understanding of the relationship between distance, time and action.

空間を押さえる **Kūkan wo Osaeru (Control the Space)**

An important concept in distancing is the idea of 'making the space your shield'. Rather than engaging continuously with your opponent, you can move to create areas of open space (Kūkan) that allow you to attack freely but restrict the opponent's ability to counter. In this way, Kūkan (space) becomes directly related to Kuzushi (breaking balance) by moving yourself into positions in which the opponent is off-balance or wrong-footed.

受け流し Uke Nagashi (Flowing Parry)

Uke Nagashi is the technique of parrying the opponent's punches and kicks with a connected, flowing motion of your arm and body. As your opponent attacks, first evade with Tai-Sabaki, then as the opponent's strike reaches its full-extension, parry it with your arm.

上段受 Jōdan-Uke (High Parry)

As the opponent attacks with a punch at your face, evade diagonally and roll your leading hand around and up to parry. This can be done to the inside or outside of the attack.

Figure 1.6.1 Jōdan Uke

下段受 Gedan-Uke (Low Parry)

As the opponent attacks with a punch or kick at your body, evade diagonally and roll your leading hand around and down to parry the attack. This can be done to the inside or outside of the attack.

Figure 1.6.2 Gedan Uke

十文字受 **Jūmonji-Uke (Crossed Wrist Parry)**

As the opponent attacks with a punch at your face, evade to the side and cross your arms at the wrist to catch the opponent's punch between them.

This can be done to the inside or outside of the attack.

Figure 1.6.3 Jumonji Uke

7

UKEMI (BREAKFALLING)

受身

In the martial arts, Ukemi refers to the art of falling safely.

The Ukemi of Budō Taijutsu is more than just a means of preventing injury from a fall or recovering balance that has been lost. It utilises Taihenjutsu (changing body art) to receive the opponent's attack in such a way that one's balance is maintained, and it is possible, within the Ukemi, to a counter or draw a weapon.

Start by learning to roll forwards, backwards and sideways from sitting on the ground.

Next, practice from standing with just one hand touching the floor.

Once this has been mastered, learn to roll with no-hands and rolling while holding or drawing a weapon.

Roll with the feeling that the body has no corners. It is important to relax and co-ordinate your roll with your breathing.

A roll should be a controlled movement, do not try to fling yourself over by using momentum. Study in a way so that you can roll slowly and in a controlled manner.

前方廻転受身 Zenpō Kaiten (Forward Roll)

Example 1

Start in a position with your hands and knees on the floor. Lift your left knee to your chest and extend your left hand forward while engaging your core muscles to stabilise.

In time with placing your left knee on the floor, straighten your right leg and bring your left hand under as if to touch your right toe. Breathe out and relax the body to allow it to roll naturally.

You should roll from the back of your shoulder blade and across the broad area of your back. Repeat on the opposite side.

Figure 1.7.1: Zenpō Kaiten from kneeling

Example 2

From a standing position, while keeping your back straight and core muscles engaged, take a step forward with your left foot and bring your right hand to the floor as you extend your left hand forward.

Next, bring your left hand under, as if to touch your right toe, as you breathe out and relax the body to allow it to roll naturally.

You should roll from the back of your shoulder blade and across the broad area of your back.

Repeat on the opposite side.

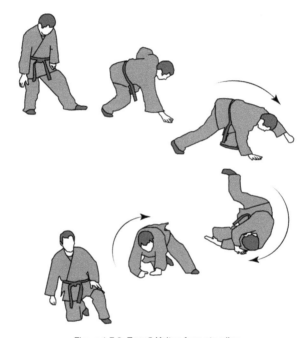

Figure 1.7.2: Zenpō Kaiten from standing

後廻転受身 Ushiro Kaiten (Backward Roll)

The backward roll is the hardest for many people to master, as it involves good core strength and flexibility to execute it in a controlled manner.

Do not fall into the trap of using momentum to fling yourself over. It is very important when practicing the back roll not to roll across your neck or the back of your head, as this can be extremely dangerous.

From a standing position, take a step back with your right foot and shift your weight across to it. Cross-step back with your left foot so that it is placed behind your right and bring both of your hands to the ground to your right as you lower yourself in a controlled manner by bending your left knee and allowing your right leg to slide along the floor directly in front of you.

Keep your body stable as you lower yourself down, still standing on your left foot with your right hip almost touching the floor and bringing your head as close to your right knee as possible by crunching your abdominal muscles.

Next, lie back as you breathe out and relax the body to allow it to roll naturally across the broad area of your back. As you roll, turn your head to the left, allowing your muscles to curl up a little further, until you can place your right foot on the floor beyond your left shoulder and complete the roll.

Repeat on the opposite side.

Figure 1.7.3: Ushiro Kaiten Ukemi

横流 Yoko Nagare (Sideways Flowing Roll)

From a standing position, cross-step with your right foot so that it is placed behind your left foot. Bend your right knee to lower yourself directly down on your right leg while keeping your shoulders square to the front.

Allow your left leg to slide along the floor directly to your right. You may place your hands down in front but keep your body stable as you lower yourself down, still standing on your right foot with your left hip almost touching the floor.

Your left leg will push further sideways until you roll across your back from your left shoulder to your right shoulder – your left leg is straight and rotates around like the hand of a clock. Repeat on the opposite side.

When practicing, ensure that your hip doesn't hit the ground. The roll should be smooth and flowing - but avoid dropping into it. Learn to control the descent by stabilising your back and core muscles and keeping your balance centred over your supporting leg.

Figure 1.7.4: Yoko-Nagare

Yoko Nagare Version 2 - Leg behind

From a standing position, cross-step with your left foot so that it is placed in front of your right foot. Bend your left knee to lower yourself directly down on your left leg while keeping your shoulders square to the front.

Allow your right leg to slide along the floor to your left, behind your left leg. You may place your hands down in front but keep your body stable as you lower yourself down, still standing on your left foot until your right hip is almost touching the floor.

Next, lie back as you breathe out and relax the body to allow it to roll naturally across the broad area of your back. As you roll, turn your head to the left, allowing your muscles to curl up a little further until you can place your right foot on the floor beyond your left shoulder and complete the roll.

Repeat on the opposite side.

Figure 1.7.5: Yoko-Nagare - Leg Behind

前方受身 Zenpō Ukemi (Forward Breakfall)

When falling forward, the natural reaction of most untrained people is to extend their hands forward, which can easily result in a broken wrist. Zenpō Ukemi allows you to take a fall forward safely.

Hold your arms in front of you at forty-five-degree angles with your palms facing forward. Your fingers should be held together and your hands close, but not touching.

Figure 1.7.6: Zenpō Ukemi hand position

From this position, allow your body to relax and fall as close to your feet as possible. Maintain your arm position, so that you land on your forearms and palms simultaneously. As you fall, swing one leg up to counterbalance.

There should be little noise or impact.

Figure 1.7.7: Zenpō Ukemi

自然行雲流水 Shizen Gyōun-Ryūsui (Natural Flow)

From your initial study of taking Ukemi on the mat, you should proceed to practice Ukemi naturally through receiving techniques from your training partners.

Shizen Gyōun-Ryūsui ("The Natural Flow of Clouds and Water") is a poetic expression referring to the art of taking Ukemi naturally, receiving the technique and going with the flow in a controlled manner. Clouds and water do not resist an obstruction but merely flow around it; your Ukemi too should ultimately flow like clouds and water.

Practicing rolls and breakfalling on a mat in class is only the first step in learning Ukemi, the next is learning to receive real techniques in training with a partner. Historically, the student may not study any actual technique for a year or more but would simply learn to take Ukemi from the technique of his teacher and senior students.

A Japanese teacher once noted that people today are in too much of a rush to learn techniques when it is far more important in the beginning just to learn to receive techniques and absorb them through your body via Ukemi.

It is important to know your limits and use caution so as not to become injured, work slowly towards natural Ukemi until you can remain relaxed and confident when you take a fall.

受身型体変術 Ukemi Gata Taihenjutsu

The Ukemi Gata Taihenjutsu is a list classifying the basic methods of rolling, somersaults and cartwheels, breakfalls, counters, and leaping techniques within Budō Taijutsu. Each of these should ultimately be mastered individually and in combination from every direction.

Ukemi should be trained slowly and only taught by an experienced instructor. It is important to know your level and not to try and jump ahead too quickly; otherwise you are risking serious injury.

前返り Mae-Gaeri (Forwards)

前方廻転 Zenpō Kaiten (Forward Roll)

1. *Two-hands*

2. *One-hand (left & right)*

3. *No-hands*

飛鳥廻転 Hichō Kaiten ("Flying Bird" Somersaults)

1. *空転 Kūten (Somersault): Two-hand; One-hand (left and right)*

2. *横転 Ōten (Cartwheel): Two-hand; One-hand (left and right)*

3. *飛び廻転 Tobi Kaiten (Dive Roll)*

自然 Shizen "Natural"

横返り Yoko-gaeri (Sideways)

側方廻転 Sokuhō Kaiten (Sideways Roll)

1. *Right*

2. *Left*

飛鳥廻転 Hichō Kaiten ("Flying Bird" Somersaults)

1. *空転 Kūten (Somersault): Two-hand; One-hand (left and right)*

2. *横転 Ōten (Cartwheel): Two-hand; One-hand (left and right)*

3. *飛び廻転 Tobi Kaiten (Dive Roll)*

自然 Shizen "Natural"

後返し Ushiro-Gaeshi (Backwards)

後方廻転 Kōhō Kaiten (Backward Roll)

1. *Two-hands*

2. *One-hand (left and right)*

3. *No-hands*

飛鳥廻転 Hichō Kaiten ("Flying Bird" Somersaults)

1. 空転 *Kūten (Somersault): Two-hand; One-hand (left and right)*

2. 横転 *Ōten (Cartwheel): Two-hand; One-hand (left and right)*

3. 飛び廻転 *Tobi Kaiten (Dive Roll)*

自然 Shizen "Natural"

前方受身 Zenpō Ukemi (Forward Breakfall)

From Kneeling

1. *Zenpō Ukemi with both hands*

2. *Zenpō Ukemi with one hand*

From Standing

1. *Zenpō Ukemi with both hands*

2. *Punch or kick after Ukemi*

自然 Shizen "Natural"

流水 Ryūsui (Flowing Water)

1. 垂流 *Tare Nagare ("Flowing Drop" Rear Breakfall)*

2. 横流 *Yoko Nagare ("Flowing Sideways" Side Breakfall)*

3. 巴返し *Tomoe-Gaeshi (Tomoe-Nage counter)*

4. 車返し *Kuruma-Gaeshi (Kuruma-Nage counter)*

5. 自然の手 *Shizen no Te (Natural Techniques)*

四方天地飛び Shihō Tenchi Tobi (Leaping)

1. 四方飛び *Shihō Tobi (Four Directional Leaping)*

2. 天地飛び *Tenchi Tobi ("Heaven Earth" Up and Down Leaping)*

3. 円飛び *Maru Tobi (Circular Leaping)*

8

GYAKU WAZA (JOINT LOCKS)

逆技

Gyaku-Waza (also known as Kansetsu-Waza) are techniques that place pressure or torque to the joints to dislocate, immobilise or take the opponent to the ground.

When Gyaku-Waza are used in combination with the basic principles of Taijutsu, very little strength or force is required to make them effective.

Flexible Balance

If I were to make a life-size statue of a person out of concrete, although the weight would be much heavier than a human being, it would be extremely easy to tip over, as any structure I build with only two legs will be unstable.

The reason we can maintain our stability, despite balancing on two legs, is because the human body is not rigid and contains over 200 movable joints. Flexible balance refers to the ability of a person to maintain their balance by making small adjustments to their posture. When pushed or pulled, your neurological system will fire up to unconsciously adjust your posture and avoid losing your balance.

By applying torsion to a joint, we can lock it up and prevent it from moving. Torsion applied simultaneously to multiple joints on the opponent's body will prevent him from making adjustments to maintain his balance.

When most people think of Gyaku-Waza, they think only of a lock applied to a single joint such as the wrist, elbow or shoulder. However, the effectiveness of a lock that is applied only to a single joint is limited against a stronger opponent, an opponent with a high pain tolerance or an opponent with very flexible joints.

Rather than applying 100% of our force against a single joint, we focus our attention on controlling the whole of the opponent's flexible balance structure by distributing the force simultaneously over multiple joints on his body.

No matter how large the opponent's body, when standing, he is still only connected to the ground by the soles of his feet. When applying a lock to a joint, your focus should not be on the joint itself but how the power is transmitted through your opponent's body and progressively lock each joint in sequence down to his feet.

Understanding the transmission of power at a basic level can be compared to the transmission of a signal, electricity or the flow of water in that we require a clear pathway and need to eliminate any inefficiency that may stop or dissipate the flow.

Example 1: Omote-Gyaku (Outward Wrist Twist)

As an example, let us examine the technique Omote-Gyaku, in which the wrist is twisted outward to bring the opponent down to the floor.

Figure 1.8.1: Example 1: Omote-Gyaku

Rather than using Omote-Gyaku only to apply pressure on the single joint of the opponent's wrist, by aligning your body correctly, Omote-Gyaku also locks the opponent's elbow joint, shoulder, the vertebrae down his spine, his pelvis, knees and ankles.

Example 2: Ura-Gyaku (Inward Wrist Twist)

We can examine this principle further through the basic technique Ura-Gyaku, in which the wrist is twisted inward to bring the opponent forward and down to the floor.

The opponent's flexible balance system is cut off by first applying torsion to his wrist while aligning your body in such a way that your opponent's elbow, shoulder, spine, pelvis, hips, knees and feet are locked up in sequence.

The key is to align yourself to transmit the power to lock up each joint in sequence by creating a clear pathway and not allow the control to be stopped or dissipated.

Figure 1.8.2: Example 2: Ura-Gyaku

Body Structure and the Power Delivery System

When coming to grips with an opponent, ensure you maintain a good posture. Keep your hands relaxed and soft, as a strong grip makes your hands and forearms stiff and unresponsive, allowing your opponent to easily counter your techniques.

Power is generated by first stepping with your foot, then shifting your body weight across to it as you twist your shoulders and hips. The hands and arms are used only as conduits to deliver the power to the opponent's joints.

If you extend your arms to grab or control, your opponent will be able to easily counter you by controlling your elbows. To avoid this, always keep your elbows close to your body.

When a technique is not working in training, rather than trying harder and more forcefully, it is better to go slower and softer to sense the point at which you are losing connection and identify why the power is not being correctly transferred to your opponent. This approach can be compared to slowly rotating a handle of a machine until you feel the cogs of the mechanism engage.

逆技 Gyaku-Waza (Joint Locks)

When training in Gyaku-Waza, avoid falling into the trap of focussing only on the joint you are trying to lock and lose sight of a potential counter by your opponent. Maintain a posture so that you can change to defend, strike or draw a weapon as necessary.

Beyond the basic Gyaku-Waza detailed in this chapter, there are many variations and combinations of Gyaku-Waza applied with Nage-Waza and Atekomi.

親殺 Oya-Goroshi

Bring the palm of your hand to the opponent's thumb and push in to apply the lock.

Figure 1.8.3: Oya-Goroshi

子殺 **Ko-Goroshi**

Push your thumb into the space between the opponent's ring and little fingers. Grasp his little finger to apply the lock.

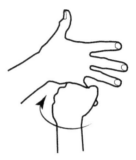

Figure 1.8.4: Ko-Goroshi

表逆 **Omote-Gyaku**

Place your thumb on the back of the opponent's hand and rotate the wrist outward. You may also place the thumb or palm of your opposite hand on the back of the opponent's hand to reinforce the lock.

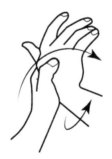

Figure 1.8.5: Omote-Gyaku

裏逆 Ura-Gyaku

Place your palm on the back of the opponent's hand and rotate the wrist inward. You may also control the opponent's elbow with your opposite hand.

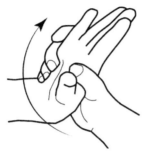

Figure 1.8.6: Ura-Gyaku

本逆 Hon-Gyaku

Place your palm on the back of the opponent's hand to hold it vertically, with his thumb facing down and his little finger facing upward. You may also bring your opposite hand to his palm to reinforce the lock. Apply pressure downwards.

Figure 1.8.7: Hon-Gyaku

表竹折 Omote-Take-Ori

Place the palm of your hand on the palm of the opponent's hand with your thumb and forefinger encircling his wrist. Fold his hand towards his forearm to apply the lock.

Figure 1.8.8: Omote-Take-Ori

裏竹折 Ura-Take-Ori

Place the palm of your hand on the back of the opponent's hand with your thumb and forefinger encircling his wrist. Fold the wrist towards his forearm to apply the lock.

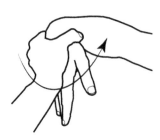

Figure 1.8.9: Ura-Take-Ori

武者捕 **Musha-Dori**

Rotate your arm over and around the opponent's arm from the outside, turning it back in and under his elbow, to capture his arm in a bent-arm lock with your forearm beneath his elbow. You may also clasp your hand together with your opposite hand to reinforce the lock.

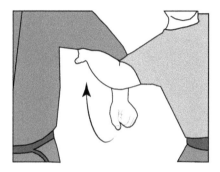

Figure 1.8.10: Musha-Dori

武双捕 **Musō-Dori**

Rotate your arm under and around the opponent's arm from the outside, to capture his arm in a straight-arm lock with your hand placed at his elbow joint. You may also clasp your hand together with your opposite hand to reinforce the lock.

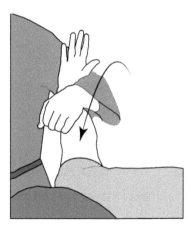

Figure 1.8.11: Musō-Dori

表鬼砕 Omote-Oni-Kudaki

Capture the opponent's arm in a bent-arm lock with one arm at the inside of his wrist and the opposite from behind his upper arm. Clasp your hands together as illustrated, to reinforce the lock.

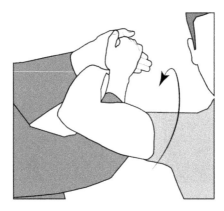

Figure 1.8.12: Omote-Oni-Kudaki

裏鬼砕 Ura-Oni-Kudaki

Capture the opponent's arm in a bent-arm lock with one arm at the inside of his wrist and the opposite placed over the top of the inside of his elbow joint.

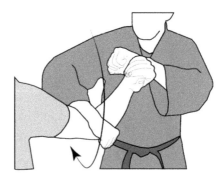

Figure 1.8.13: Ura-Oni-Kudaki

大逆 Ō-Gyaku

Place one hand at the opponent's shoulder and the opposite at his wrist as you rotate the arm in a big motion to apply a lock to his shoulder joint.

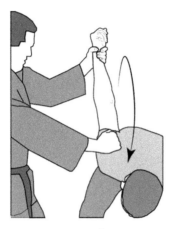

Figure 1.8.14: Ō-Gyaku

9

NAGE WAZA (THROWING TECHNIQUES)

投技

Nage-Waza (throwing techniques) are not applied forcefully but utilise the flow of movement and the Kūkan (space) to place the opponent at a point of disequilibrium from which he cannot recover. When Nage-Waza are applied, it should appear as if the opponent has thrown himself.

崩し Kuzushi (Unbalancing)

To throw an opponent, it is first necessary to upset his balance with Kuzushi. Nage-Waza are applied in different ways according to the specific technique, but fundamental to any throw is first bringing the opponent off balance, then applying the power of the whole body in a unified motion. If the opponent can recover his balance when you attempt to apply a throwing technique, then the Kuzushi was insufficient.

The power of both the Kuzushi and the Nage-Waza are provided by the coordinated action of the body working as one unit, concentrated on the opponent's weakest line of balance. The power of your whole body is transmitted to the opponent through your arms; however, it is important not to solely use the power of your arms to apply the technique as this can be easily sensed and countered by the opponent.

To understand balance, first imagine that you were to draw a box on the floor around your feet to represent your base. Next, imagine you hung a small weight on a piece of string from your belt to represent your centre of gravity. As you then lean your body in different directions, you would find that as long as your centre of gravity sits within the box, you will be in good balance, but as soon as your centre of gravity falls outside of the box, you will become unstable.

By widening your feet and lowering your centre of gravity, you may increase the area of your base but will remain relatively unstable if you lean towards your shortest baseline direction. This will remain true regardless of how you place your feet.

To understand the relationship between your foot position and balance, we can examine the following experiment: place three matchboxes on a book, as illustrated, then raise one side of the book.

'Matchbox B' with the shortest base and highest centre of gravity will fall first.

Although 'Matchbox A' has the lower centre of gravity, it will fall soon after 'Matchbox B".

'Matchbox C' has the longest baseline dimension and is, therefore, the most stable so will fall last or slide off the book before it falls at all.

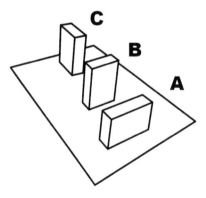

Figure 1.9.1: Baseline dimension and stability

We can observe from this experiment that Kuzushi is best applied against the shortest baseline distance.

踵線 Kakato-Sen (The Heel Line)

The Kakato-Sen represents a line between the opponent's heels. When he places his feet apart, it is the longest baseline dimension and therefore the most stable.

弱線 Jyaku-Sen (The Weak Line)

The Jyaku-Sen represents a line at ninety-degrees to the Kakato-Sen and the opponent's shortest baseline dimension. The Jyaku-Sen is the line in which you should apply your Kuzushi.

In the following illustration, the Kakato-Sen is represented by a solid line and the Jyaku-Sen by a dashed line.

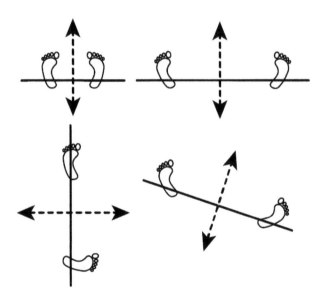

Figure 1.9.2: Kakuto-Sen and Jyaku-Sen

The relationship between the Kakato-Sen and Jyaku-Sen remains the same regardless of how the opponent places his feet or if your opponent is moving or standing still. If the opponent is moving, the direction of the Jyaku-Sen will change with each adjustment of his foot position. It is therefore important to harmonise with his movement when applying Kuzushi.

Kuzushi Method 1: Direct

The first and simplest type of Kuzushi emerges when the opponent's unbalanced condition is achieved by the application of a direct movement. This can be achieved in two ways:

The opponent carelessly places himself in an unstable position, becomes unbalanced, is startled or struck so as he is momentarily knocked off balance. You can capitalise on the unbalanced state by driving the Kuzushi further and then applying the throw.

A direct Kuzushi can also be created by skilfully applying the movement of your whole body in one action to unbalance and then throw your opponent. Although a direct Kuzushi can be used successfully, this method is difficult to achieve against a larger, stronger and more athletic opponent and contains a considerable risk of being countered.

Kuzushi Method 2: Indirect

Indirect Kuzushi occurs when the unbalanced condition of the opponent is achieved by employing two or more actions. Through deception and the outmanoeuvring of your opponent, more successful results can be obtained by indirect rather than direct methods of Kuzushi.

The simplest and most common method of indirect Kuzushi is called the "action-reaction" method.

The opponent is first brought from a state of balance to unbalance, he then attempts to regain his lost balance by reacting strongly in the opposite direction. Using the coordinated power of your whole body, you utilise his reaction to accelerate his state of unbalance into the direction of his reaction and throw him.

As an example, to throw the opponent forward with Ippon-Seoi-Nage, you may first push directly against him, causing his balance to be lost to his rear. The opponent will then usually react by pushing back against your push in an effort to regain his balance. Utilising the opponent's push forward, you then harmonise with it to reverse the direction into a pulling motion, accelerating the forward momentum beyond what the opponent intended, causing him to become severely unbalanced to the front. From this point, you simply turn the body to enter to the Ippon-Seoi-Nage position and guide the opponent over to complete the throw.

Figure 1.9.3: Action-Reaction

投技 Nage Waza (Throwing Techniques)

For Nage-Waza, the Kuzushi contributes at least ninety percent to the success, but numerous trainees place little attention to it and concentrate only on the throwing action itself. If your mind is only focussed on the opponent hitting the mat, you will never learn to throw effectively. Use Kuzushi first to successfully unbalance your opponent before entering in for the Nage-Waza.

When executing a throw, it is necessary to maintain posture, balance and control of the opponent throughout. Maintain your posture so that you can defend against a counter, strike or draw a weapon as necessary.

Beyond the basic categories of Nage-Waza detailed in this chapter lies a kaleidoscope of variations. The first step is to master the basic techniques, then work on combinations, variations and combining Gyaku-Waza and Atekomi in application.

巌石投 Ganseki Nage

Unbalance the opponent by shifting his weight directly forward on his toes or diagonally to the little toe on his right-front corner. Fit your body into his by stepping in deeply with your right foot and pivot in front of him so as your right arm hooks under his left shoulder or elbow. Throw him by projecting your body forward as you rotate slightly from the hips. Your right arm should remain neutral, do not use it to apply pressure or twist - the throw comes from the body, not the arm.

Figure 1.9.4: Ganseki Nage

巌石落 Ganseki Otoshi

Unbalance the opponent by shifting his weight directly forward on his toes. Fit your body into his by stepping in deeply with your right foot and pivot in front of him as your right arm hooks under his left shoulder or elbow. Drop him directly downwards by sliding your right foot back against his left leg as you lower your body forward and down. Your right arm should remain neutral, do not use it to apply pressure or twist - it is your body that should do the work, not the arm.

Figure 1.9.5: Ganseki Otoshi

大外掛 Ōsoto-Gake

Unbalance the opponent by shifting his weight to his heels, either to his rear or right-rear corner. Fit your body in by stepping behind him with your left foot as you place your right shoulder against his left to apply pressure. Place the back of your right leg against the back of his left leg, then lower your body as you twist slightly to your left and apply further pressure with your right shoulder to crush the opponent down.

Figure 1.9.6: Ōsoto-Gake

小外掛 Ko-Soto-Gake

Unbalance the opponent by shifting his weight to his heels, either to his rear or right-rear corner. Fit your body in by placing your left leg against the back of his right leg and lock your heel against his. Place your right shoulder against his left and crush the opponent down by lowering your body as you are twisting slightly to your left to apply further pressure with your right shoulder.

Figure 1.9.7: Ko-Soto-Gake

小内掛 Ko-Uchi-Gake

Unbalance the opponent by shifting his weight to his heels, either to his rear or right-rear corner. Fit your body in by placing the back of your right leg against the back of his right leg from the inside and lock your heel against his. Place your right shoulder against his left and crush the opponent down by lowering your body as you twist slightly to your left and apply further pressure with your right shoulder.

Figure 1.9.8: Ko-Uchi-Gake

大内掛 Ō-Uchi-Gake

Unbalance the opponent by shifting his weight to his heels, either to his rear or left-rear corner. Fit your body in by placing the back of your right leg against the back of his left leg from the inside and lock your heel against his. Place your right shoulder against his right and crush the opponent down by lowering your body as you twist slightly to your right and apply further pressure with your shoulders.

Figure 1.9.9: Ō-Uchi-Gake

双手刈 **Morote-Gari**

Unbalance the opponent by shifting his weight to his heels. Step in deeply with your right foot as you drop low and fit your body in by placing your right shoulder against his lower abdomen and your hands hooking behind his lower legs. Crush the opponent down by lowering your body as you twist slightly to your left and apply further pressure with your shoulders.

Figure 1.9.10: Morote-Gari

内股 **Uchi-Mata**

Unbalance the opponent by shifting his weight directly forward on his toes or diagonally to his right-front corner to his little toe. Fit your body in by pivoting in front of him so as your right hip makes contact with his mid-section. Lift your right leg up between his legs as you pull his balance forward by twisting your body slightly to your left. Spring up with your left leg as you lift your right leg high up between the opponent's legs to throw in a circular motion.

Figure 1.9.11: Uchi-Mata

腰投 Koshi-Nage

Unbalance the opponent by shifting his weight directly forward on his toes or diagonally to his right-front corner to his little toe. Fit your body in by pivoting in front of him so as your arm encircles his waist and your right hip makes contact with his mid-section as you roll him up onto your lower back. Pull his balance further forward by twisting your body slightly to your left as you spring up with your hips to throw him in a circular motion.

Figure 1.9.12: Koshi-Nage

瀧落 **Taki Otoshi (variation):** As the opponent is lifted in the air for Koshi-Nage, leap out and drive the opponent's body straight down to the ground so that he is unable to take Ukemi.

大外投 **Ōsoto-Nage**

Unbalance the opponent by shifting his weight to his right heel. Fit your body in by stepping behind him with your left, then right foot and pivot your hips behind him so as they make contact below your opponent's right hip. Throw the opponent over your right hip by rotating your body downward to your left as you spring your hips up.

Figure 1.9.13: Ōsoto-Nage

拂腰 **Harai-Goshi**

Unbalance the opponent by shifting his weight to his little toe on the right-front corner. Fit your body in by pivoting in front of him so your right hip makes contact with the centre of his abdomen. Sweep his right leg up with your right leg as you throw him over your right hip by twisting your body to your left as you spring up with your left leg to throw him in a circular motion.

Figure 1.9.14: Harai-Goshi

跳腰投 Hane-Goshi-Nage

Unbalance the opponent by shifting his weight to his little toe on the right-front corner. Fit your body in by pivoting in front of him so that your right hip makes contact with the centre of his abdomen. Bend your right knee and place it on the inside of the opponent's right leg as you twist your body to your left and spring up with your left leg to lift him off the mat with the coordinated action of your right leg and hip. The opponent should turn over your right hip for the throw. When placing your right leg, ensure that your right knee is placed past the opponent's right leg to establish contact with your leg, hip and chest to the opponent.

Figure 1.9.15: Hane-Goshi-Nage

背負投 Seoi-Nage

Unbalance the opponent by shifting his weight directly forward on his toes. Fit your body in by pivoting in front of the opponent so as your back is against his chest. Drive your right elbow up under the opponent's right arm with your right palm facing upwards so as your right forearm fits under his armpit. Pull the opponent's balance further forward by twisting your body slightly to your left as you spring up with your hips against his thighs to throw.

Figure 1.9.16: Seoi-Nage

一本背負投 Ippon-Seoi-Nage

Unbalance the opponent by shifting his weight directly forward on his toes. Fit your body in by pivoting in front of the opponent so as your back is against his chest. Your right arm hooks under his right arm with your right shoulder fitting under his armpit. Pull the opponent's balance further forward by twisting your body slightly to your left as you spring up with your hips against his thighs to throw.

Figure 1.9.17: Ippon-Seoi-Nage

逆背負投 Gyaku-Seoi-Nage

Unbalance the opponent by shifting his weight directly forward on his toes. Fit your body in by pivoting in front of the opponent so as your left hip sits against right hip. Your left arm hooks under his right arm from the outside with your right shoulder fitting under his armpit. Pull the opponent's balance further forward by twisting your body slightly to your right as you spring up with your hips against his thighs to throw him forward.

Figure 1.9.18: Gyaku-Seoi-Nage

瀧落 **Taki Otoshi (variation):** For Seoi-Nage, Ippon-Seoi-Nage and Gyaku-Seoi-Nage: as the opponent is lifted in the air, leap out and drive the opponent's body straight down to the ground so that he is unable to take Ukemi.

片手投 Katate-Nage

Unbalance the opponent by catching his right hand or wrist from the outside and shift his weight directly forward on his toes or diagonally to his little toe in the right-front corner. Lift the opponent's right arm high as you step under, coming out to his left side. Drop to your left knee and turn your body to your left to pull the opponent's balance further forward and throw him.

Figure 1.9.19: Katate-Nage

巴投 Tomoe-Nage

Unbalance the opponent by shifting his weight directly forward on his toes. Step deeply with your left foot between his legs, bend your left knee and sit back as you slide your left hip as close to your left foot as possible. Simultaneously, bend your right knee and place your right foot on the opponent's lower abdomen, at his left hip. Throw by straightening your right leg as you pull the opponent over the top of you.

Figure 1.9.20: Tomoe-Nage

横巴投 Yoko-Tomoe-Nage

Unbalance the opponent by shifting his weight directly forward on his toes or diagonally to his left-front corner to his little toe. Step deeply with your left foot between his legs, bend your left knee and sit back as you slide your left hip as close to your left foot as possible. Simultaneously, bend your right knee and place your right foot on the opponent's lower abdomen, at his left hip. Rotate to your right side so as you bring your right armpit to the outside of the opponent's left ankle. Straighten your right leg as you pull to throw him in a circular motion to your right.

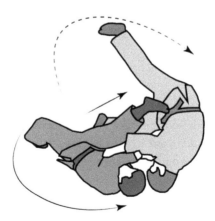

Figure 1.9.21: Yoko-Tomoe-Nage

立流 Tachi-Nagare

Unbalance the opponent by shifting his weight directly forward on his toes. Step deeply with your left foot between his legs, bend your left knee and sit back as you slide your left hip as close to your left foot as possible. Simultaneously, bend your right knee and place the instep of your right foot to the back of the opponent's left knee and the instep of your left foot to the back of the opponent's right knee. Throw by straightening your legs diagonally outward as you pull the opponent over the top of you.

Figure 1.9.22: Tachi-Nagare

横流 Yoko-Nagare

Unbalance the opponent by shifting his weight directly forward on his toes or diagonally to his left-front corner to his little toe. Step deeply with your right foot to your right, bend your right knee and sit back as you slide your left foot along the floor, bringing your right hip as close to your right foot as possible. Your left hip should sit against the opponent's left ankle as you turn your body to your right and pull the opponent over the top of you.

Figure 1.9.23: Yoko-Nagare

手枕 Te-Makura

Unbalance the opponent by shifting his weight directly forward on his toes. Grasp the opponent's right wrist with your left hand and scoop up from below his right elbow with your right arm. Place your right hand behind your head and turn your left shoulder to your right to lock the opponent's right elbow as you place your right shin in front of his right shin. Bend both knees and sit back as you slide your hips as close to your feet as possible. Throw by straightening your right leg as you pull the opponent over to throw.

Figure 1.9.24: Te-Makura

車投 Kuruma-Nage

Kuruma Nage can be executed from Tomoe-Nage, Yoko-Tomoe-Nage, Tachi-Nagare, Yoko-Nagare or Te-Makura. As the throw is executed, and the opponent rolls over the top of you, roll along with him to finish sitting on top and hold him down.

Figure 1.9.25: Kuruma-Nage

10

SHIME WAZA (CONSTRICTION TECHNIQUES)

絞技

Shime-Waza are techniques that either:

- Strangle by compressing the carotid arteries and / or jugular veins, thus restricting the flow of blood and oxygen to the brain.
- Choke by compressing the upper airway (trachea or larynx) causing asphyxia.
- Compress the chest or lungs to prevent breathing.

When correctly applied, Shime-Waza may lead to unconsciousness within ten to twenty seconds and if held for an extended length of time may also lead to serious injury or death. Generally, strangulation techniques that restrict the flow of blood are considered superior to choking techniques applied to the throat, as these require considerably less physical strength to apply.

It is important when applying Shime-Waza not to put tension into your arms but keep them soft and relaxed. The successful application relies on accuracy, not strength.

For Shime-Waza applied from the front, such as Hon-Jime, Gyaku-Jime and Itami-Jime, the most common position of application is when holding the opponent down in Uma-Nori.

馬乗り **Uma Nori**

Pin the opponent to the floor on his back by sitting astride him with your knees under his armpits and your centre of gravity kept low. From this position, you can make adjustments to your posture to control his movement and prevent his escape.

Figure 1.10.1: Uma Nori

本締 **Hon-Jime (Basic Choke)**

Grasp the opponent's lower left lapel with your left hand, then take a grip with your right hand on his upper right lapel with the thumb on the inside of his collar. Pull with your left hand and apply the choke by turning your right wrist in an action similar to as if you are opening a jar. You should be applying pressure to the artery on the right side of the opponent's neck.

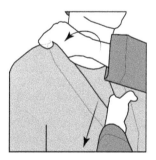

Figure 1.10.2: Hon-Jime

逆締 Gyaku-Jime (Reverse Choke)

Grasp the opponent's lower left lapel with your left hand, then take a grip with your right hand on his upper right lapel with your fingers on the inside of his collar. Pull with your left hand and apply the choke by rotating your right wrist in an action similar to as if you are opening a jar. You should be applying pressure to the artery on the right side of the opponent's neck.

Figure 1.10.3: Gyaku-Jime

痛締 Itami-Jime (Painful Choke)

Grip high on the opponent's left collar with your right hand and high on the opponent's right collar with your left hand. Apply the choke by simultaneously pushing in with your thumb joints to both sides of his neck.

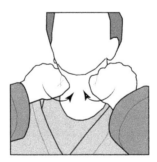

Figure 1.10.4: Itami-Jime

三角締 Sankaku-Jime (Triangle Choke)

Method One

Bring your right arm around the opponent's neck from behind and place it on the inside of your left elbow. The point of your right elbow should be in line with the opponent's chin. Place your left hand behind the opponent's head. Apply by squeezing your arms to tighten the grip as you push your head into the back of the opponent's head.

Figure 1.10.5: Sankaku-Jime Method One

Method Two

Bring your right arm around the opponent's neck from behind and grasp the opening of your left sleeve. Place your left hand behind the opponent's head, grasp your right sleeve and tighten.

Figure 1.10.6: Sankaku-Jime Method Two

洞締 Dō-Jime (Body Choke)

Hold the opponent between your legs. Push up with your feet to squeeze your knees together and restrict the breathing of the opponent. While executing Dō-Jime, use your hands to simultaneously perform Hon-Jime, Gyaku-Jime, Itami-Jime or Sankaku-Jime.

Figure 1.10.7: Dō-Jime

11

GOSHINJUTSU (SELF DEFENCE)

護身術

For the samurai of feudal Japan, the study of Bujutsu (martial technique) was fundamental to his occupation - to engage with an opponent and defeat them in combat, either on the field of battle or defending order within his lord's domain.

A samurai would walk onto the battlefield wielding his spear. Once his spear was broken, he would draw his sword; once he lost his sword, he would draw his dagger, and then once he lost that, he would grapple with his opponents unarmed. Bujutsu of that time was not a series of specialised skills but a complete system of combat.

In modern times we think of the application of Bujutsu in terms of Goshinjutsu (self-defence). Budo Taijutsu provides a practical form of self-defence that does not rely on the physical size or strength of the practitioner.

As it was for the samurai and ninja of feudal Japan, in modern self-defence there can be no certainty when or where an attack may take place, how many adversaries may be involved and how they may be armed.

In a self-defence situation, there are no weight divisions. We should always assume that our attacker will be physically larger and stronger than us, which entails that we can rule out techniques or tactics that primarily rely on strength.

In a self-defence situation, there is no gender divide. Any technique we practice should work equally well for a woman against a man.

In a self-defence situation, there is no ring or contest area. Techniques and tactics that require a large amount of floor space or only work on a flat surface need to be modified so as they can be employed in crowded, cluttered environments and on uneven surfaces.

In a self-defence situation, there are no rules. An attacker may launch a surprise attack from behind, use any sort of dirty trick and may conceal a weapon. Therefore, techniques that rely on particular types of attacks or only work under a set of contest rules can also be ruled out.

剛者捕り Gōsha-Dori

Our self-defence system is based on the knowledge of Gōsha-Dori (strongman control) which is the study of how to fight against much stronger, larger opponents.

- Never fight your opponent on an equal footing, always try to take any advantage you can and do whatever it takes to survive.
- Maintain your balance and keep the opponent off balance.
- Keep your eyes on your opponent at all times.
- Concentrate your attack on the weakest points of his body such as his fingers, eyes, groin, ribs, shins and use Happa-Ken against his ears.
- Use any object at hand as an improvised weapon.
- Use Kiai by shouting from deep in your lower abdomen, not from high in the chest. A strong Kiai gives you confidence and can cause the opponent to falter.
- Attack continuously, keep attacking until the opponent is completely incapacitated or immobilised.
- Use your surroundings to restrict the mobility of the attacker. Crowd him in a corner or knock objects down to block his path.
- Use your surroundings to facilitate your escape. Give yourself a clear exit.
- Always try to end the fight as quickly as possible.
- Maintain a calm and confident attitude. Fight back from a place of strength, not anger or fear.

Attacking a weak point (such as the eyes), without *first* controlling your opponent's mental and physical balance may just lead to an even stronger and more vicious attack from him. Self-defence is more than just learning a few tricks; you first need to train in distance and balance control to make the techniques effective.

The mindset in combat for the samurai can be expressed with "You cut my flesh, I cut your bones. You cut my bones, I cut off your life". The feeling is of accepting that you will receive damage but will attack strongly and confidently to overwhelm your attacker.

For example, when facing an attacker armed with a knife and there is no chance of escape, you attack strongly with the view of defeating him completely, regardless of whether or not you are cut or stabbed in the process.

Self-defence and survival are often more about mindset, confidence and mentally unbalancing your opponent than it is about technique.

The art of Goshinjutsu also includes the study of escapes from various grabs and holds.

手解 Te-Hodoki (Releasing the Hand)

As the opponent grabs your wrist, step in with the feeling of driving your elbow towards him. You can then break your wrist out of the space between his thumb and index finger in the direction of your thumb.

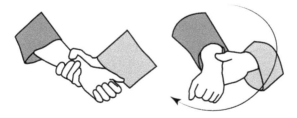

Figure 1.11.1: Te-Hodoki

Immediately follow up with a strike or grab.

There are many variations of this basic technique, such as against double wrist grabs, cross wrist grabs and wrist-elbow grabs.

体解 Tai-Hodoki (Releasing the Body)

As the opponent tries to grab around your body from behind, strike back with the rear of your head to his face as you spread your arms out, round your shoulders slightly and turn your hips to one side to escape.

Figure 1.11.2: Tai-Hodoki

Immediately follow up with a strike, joint lock or throw.

There are many variations of this basic technique, such as against grabs from the front or side, the Full-Nelson, headlock, etc.

Also, practice against an attacker attempting to hold you down on the ground in various positions using the same methodology.

腰砕 Koshi Kudaki (Defence against Throwing Techniques)

As the opponent attacks with Koshi-Nage, push against his hip with your free hand, sink your hips and release any tension from your upper body to block the throw.

Immediately follow up with a strike, joint lock or counter-throw.

There are many variations that can be applied against various different throwing techniques.

Figure 1.11.3: Koshi-Kudaki

12

MUSHIN (NO-MIND)

無心

When beginning their training in Budō Taijutsu, many people believe that they will be instructed in individual techniques to handle each situation. The problem with this approach is that there is a limit to how many techniques a person can master, but an infinite number of situations they may face.

Techniques require conscious thought, while an attack requires an immediate, natural and unconscious response.

As important as the study of technique is, it remains in the realm of conscious thought. Training must be conducted in such a way so as it is absorbed into your muscle memory to the point that it becomes your natural way of moving.

There is a lot of emphasis placed, not only in our martial tradition but also in much of Japanese culture, on the concept of not thinking but just doing. Japanese teachers will often instruct us that Budō is something to be practiced with our body and not something to be studied intellectually.

From my experience, Western students will join a Dōjō in Japan with lots of questions they want to be answered but will be advised to just train (or more pertinently to 'shut up and train').

The best way to learn anything is to engage with it fully without holding onto preconceptions or trying to intellectualise every point because once you do, you are then allowing yourself to introduce your own ideas. Once you add your own ideas, you will be more engaged with them than the very thing you are trying to learn.

意識 Ishiki (Consciousness)

The Japanese word Ishiki has many nuances, but we will look at it as meaning 'conscious attention'. Almost like a physical object, the Japanese believe that your conscious attention can reside in a particular place at any time.

As an example, if you sit in a garden and simply allow yourself to take in the whole scene without directing your conscious attention anywhere, you are free of Ishiki. If you then focus your attention on a particular tree, your Ishiki resides there. If you focus in further to a single leaf, your Ishiki resides in that leaf. If you hear a sound such as a bird, car or people talking, your Ishiki may immediately be thrown to the sound. And if you are looking at the garden but your mind is full of thoughts, it means your Ishiki is directed inwardly at those thoughts.

This relates to Budō training by allowing yourself to become aware of where your conscious attention falls.

If your Ishiki falls on your opponent's weapon or technique, you will most likely be taken in by it. For example, by directing your conscious attention to a knife stabbing at you, as you try and evade, the weapon will follow you.

If your Ishiki is directed at your own technique, it will likely almost always fail. Once your conscious attention is directed at a technique or precedes your action, your body gives off its intention to your opponent.

You also lose control of the whole situation because your focus becomes pinpointed on one thing. As an example, you may direct your conscious attention to a wrist-lock, but by focussing only on the wrist, you have no control over the rest of the opponent's body and fail to respond to his counterattack.

Worst of all is if your Ishiki is directed inwards with thoughts such as "Wow, this guy is strong!", "How did this happen?" or "What should I do next?".

虚実転換法 Kyojitsu Tenkan-Hō (Art of Deception)

Ishiki can also be used as a powerful tool *against* your opponent by drawing his conscious attention.

Very simple examples include raising your hand or giving a shout. In such cases, your opponent's consciousness is drawn to your hand or the shout and away from your actual attack.

In Ninpō (the way of the Ninja), controlling the opponent's Ishiki was an important part of Kyojitsu Tenkan-Hō (usually abbreviated to just Kyojitsu) which literally means the 'Art of the Juxtaposition of Truth and Falsehood' or simply 'The Art of Deception'.

Previously in this book, we focused on understanding and controlling the opponent's physical balance but Kyojitsu controls another equally important balance system – your opponent's mental balance.

When your opponent's mental balance is strong and he is relaxed, it is very difficult to break his physical balance or effectively apply a technique on him. Drawing the opponent's Ishiki to a point that causes fear, pain or confusion immediately destabilises him and allows for a more efficient application of technique.

無心 Mushin (No-Mind)

A major point of consideration and study for the warriors of old Japan was how we can break free of our conscious attention jumping around or falling inward to be consumed with our thoughts.

The state of Mushin is sometimes misunderstood as being a trance-like state but is actually one in which your attention is directed on everything around you but not focussed on any particular detail.

Your mind and body are fully focussed on the task without any mental chatter, your body responds and moves naturally to where it needs to be, and your mind lets go of that which would trap it.

You would be familiar with the state of Mushin when fully consumed in an interesting movie or book or when so deeply involved with a task that you lose all sense of self. You feel so into the task you are performing, you lose your sense of time and become at one with it.

In Japanese history, much was written on the correct state of mind in combat. In addition to the concept of Mushin, there were several other states described including:

- 不動心 Fudōshin (The immovable mind)
- 平常心 Heijōshin (Your normal relaxed state of mind)
- 無念無想 Munen Musō (No thoughts and no desires)

Although all these philosophical ideas contain slightly different nuances, it is beyond the scope of this book to give a detailed examination of each of them; therefore, I will group them all under the general term Mushin.

Achieving a State of Mushin

One popular way of training oneself to maintain a state of Mushin was through the practice of Zazen (Zen Meditation). In the most popular approach, the practitioner sits in a full or half-lotus position and empties the mind, not allowing it to fix on any thought.

Another method was the practice of Kuji–In (Nine Symbol Mudra) and Jūji (Ten Symbol Cutting) methods which could allow the practitioner to enter a state of Mushin at will.

Most importantly to us, was the simple act of practicing our martial art to the point where Mushin becomes our natural state of mind.

This was written as "From training with the sword, spear, staff and Jūjutsu you can enter the state of Munen Musō" (剣槍棒柔共無念夢想に入る "Ken, Sō, Bō, Yawara tomo Munen Musō ni Hairu")

Although Zazen and Kuji-In are useful supplements, the daily practice of Budō Taijutsu is still the best preparation in maintaining a state of Mushin.

PART II

KEIKO GATA (PRACTICE FORMS)

武道体術の稽古型

KIHON GATA

基本型

1

KIHON GATA: GOGYŌ NO KATA / SANSHIN NO KATA

五行の型・三心の型

地の型 Chi no Kata

1. From Shizentai.
2. I step back with my right foot, extend my left hand in front of me and place my right fist, with the thumb pointed upwards, on my right hip.
3. I then step forward with my right foot and use my right hand to thrust forward with Sanshin-Tsuki, as I pull my opposite hand back to my hip.
4. I repeat the technique on the opposite side.

Figure 2.1.1: Chi no Kata

水の型 Sui no Kata

1. From Shizentai.
2. I step back with my right foot, extend my left hand in front of me and place my right fist, with the thumb pointed upwards, on my right hip.
3. I perform Jōdan-Uke with my left hand, then step forward with my right foot and use my right hand to strike with Omote-Shutō.
4. I repeat the technique on the opposite side.

Figure 2.1.2: Sui no Kata

火の型 Ka no Kata

1. From Shizentai.
2. I step back with my right foot, extend my left hand in front of me and place my right fist, with the thumb pointed upwards, on my right hip.
3. I perform Jōdan-Uke with my left hand, then step forward with my right foot and use my right hand to strike with Ura-Shutō.
4. I repeat the technique on the opposite side.

Figure 2.1.3: Ka no Kata

風の型 Fū no Kata

1. From Shizentai.
2. I step back with my right foot, extend my left hand in front of me and place my right fist, with the thumb pointed upwards, on my right hip.
3. I perform Gedan-Uke with my left hand then step forward with my right foot and use my right hand to thrust with Shitō-ken.
4. I repeat the technique on the opposite side.

Figure 2.1.4: Fū no Kata

空の型 Kū no Kata

1. From Shizentai.
2. I step back with my right foot, extend my left hand in front of me and place my right fist, with the thumb pointed upwards, on my right hip.
3. I perform Gedan-Uke with my left hand.
4. I then raise my right hand, drop my hips and kick high with my right foot.
5. I repeat the technique on the opposite side.

Figure 2.1.5: Kū no Kata

KIHON GATA: KIHON HAPPŌ

基本八法

The Kihon Happō is made up of two parts, the Koshi Sanpō and the Torite Gohō.

骨指三法 Koshi Sanpō

一文字の構 Ichimonji no Kamae

1. I stand facing the opponent in Ichimonji no Kamae, with my half-open right hand extended in front of me and my left fist, with the thumb pointed upwards, on the inside of my right elbow.
2. The opponent attacks with a left punch to the face.
3. I evade the opponent's punch by stepping diagonally to my left with my left foot.
4. I then rotate my right hand clockwise from my left hip around and upward, while making a fist, to smash through the opponent's attacking arm with Jōdan-Uke.
5. Next, I step forward with my left foot and strike to the right side of the opponent's neck with Omote-Shutō.
6. I repeat the technique on the opposite side.

Figure 2.2.1: Ichimonji no Kamae

飛鳥の構 Hichō no Kamae

1. I stand facing the opponent in Hichō no Kamae, with my left foot at my right knee and my half-open left hand extended in front of me. I place my right fist, with the thumb pointed upwards, on the inside of my left elbow.
2. The opponent attacks with a right punch or kick to the body.
3. I make a fist with my left hand as I rotate it down to parry the opponent's attack with Gedan-Uke. My right fist remains at my left shoulder.
4. I then kick to Suigetsu with my left foot.
5. Next, I step forward with my right foot and strike to the artery on the right side of the opponent's neck with Ura-Shutō.
6. I repeat the technique on the opposite side.

Figure 2.2.2: Hichō no Kamae

右十文字の構 **Jūmonji no Kamae**

1. I stand facing the opponent in Jūmonji no Kamae with my left hand on the inside.
2. The opponent attacks with a left punch to the face.
3. I evade the opponent's punch by stepping diagonally to my left with my left foot.
4. I rotate my right hand clockwise to my upper right to parry the attack with Jōdan-Uke, then thrust forward with my right thumb to the opponent's chest.
5. I raise my half-open right hand to my upper-right as I retreat one step back.
6. The opponent attacks with a right punch to the face.
7. I evade the opponent's punch by stepping diagonally to my right with my right foot.
8. I rotate my left hand clockwise to my upper left to parry the attack with Jōdan-Uke, then thrust with my left thumb to the opponent's chest.
9. I raise my half-open left hand to my upper-left as I retreat one step back and return to Jūmonji no Kamae.
10. I repeat the technique on the opposite side.

Figure 2.2.3: Jūmonji no Kamae

捕手五法 Torite Gohō

表小手型 Omote Kote Gata

1. The opponent grabs my left lapel with his right hand.
2. I cover his grabbing hand with my left, lower my hips, twist my spine and turn my left elbow towards his as I push upward to break his right-hand grip.
3. I then lift the opponent's right hand high with my left, take a step back with my left foot as I turn to my left to apply Omote-Gyaku.
4. I repeat the technique on the opposite side.

Figure 2.2.4: Omote Kote Gata

表逆券捌型 Omote Gyaku Ken Sabaki Gata

1. The opponent grabs my right lapel with his left hand and punches to my face with his right.
2. I cover the opponent's grabbing hand with my right, step diagonally back with my right foot and parry his punch with my left hand.
3. I then lower my hips as I push upward to break the opponent's left-hand grip and apply Omote-Gyaku.
4. I repeat the technique on the opposite side.

Figure 2.2.5: Omote Gyaku Ken Sabaki Gata

裏小手型 Ura Kote Gata

1. The opponent grabs my left lapel with his right hand.
2. I take the opponent's grabbing hand with my right in Ura-Gyaku as I step back with my right foot to apply the lock.
3. Next, I change direction by stepping back with my left foot and

turning the opponent's wrist around from above to throw him with Omote-Gyaku.

4. I repeat the technique on the opposite side.

Figure 2.2.6: Ura Kote Gata

腕締足折型 Ude-Jime Ashi-Ori Gata

1. The opponent grabs my left sleeve at my elbow with his right hand.
2. I step to my left with my left foot.
3. I then step in as I wrap up the opponent's grabbing arm in a big motion from above to capture it in Musha-Dori.
4. I kick to the opponent's knee joint with my left foot, causing him to fall on his back.
5. I repeat the technique on the opposite side.

Figure 2.2.7: Ude-Jime Ashi-Ori Gata

巖石型 Ganseki Gata

1. The opponent grabs my right sleeve at my elbow with his left hand.
2. I step to my right with my right foot.
3. I then wrap up the opponent's grabbing arm in a big motion from below to capture it in Musō-Dori.
4. I then turn to my left to throw the opponent with Ganseki-Nage.
5. I repeat the technique on the opposite side.

Figure 2.2.8: Ganseki Gata

3

KIHON GATA: TAIHENJUTSU MUTO DORI KATA
体変術無刀捕型

平の構 Hira no Kamae

1. The opponent holds a Daitō (long sword) in Daijōdan no Kamae, with his sword free to cut straight down or horizontally at my torso.
2. I stand facing the opponent in Hira no Kamae (Shizentai) at a distance of three Shaku (approx. one metre) and remain in this position, facing the opponent, until he cuts in.
3. The moment the opponent cuts, I step back with my right foot and roll over my right shoulder to escape, returning to a standing position.

一文字の構 Ichimonji no Kamae

1. The opponent holds a Daitō in Daijōdan no Kamae, with his sword free to cut straight down or horizontally at my torso.
2. I stand facing the opponent in Ichimonji no Kamae.
3. At the moment he cuts, I roll to his left at a position three Shaku away and return to a standing position.
4. At the instant the opponent corrects his position to cut at again, I leap in, placing my left knee on the ground and strike to Suigetsu with my right thumb.

十文字 Jūmonji no Kamae

1. The opponent holds a Daitō in Daijōdan no Kamae. I stand facing the opponent in Jūmonji no Kamae.
2. The opponent attacks from Daijōdan by cutting in freely from any direction.
3. I turn my body and leap diagonally back with my left foot to my left to evade.
4. Next, I leap forward with my left foot as I pull back my right foot and strike with a left Ura-Shutō.
5. I then immediately switch my feet and strike with a right Ura-Shutō to the opposite side of the opponent's neck.

Figure 2.3.1: Hira no Kamae

Figure 2.3.2: Ichimonji no Kamae

Figure 2.3.3: Jūmonji no Kamae

SHINDEN FUDŌ RYŪ DAKENTAIJUTSU

神傳不動流打拳体術

4

SHINDEN FUDŌ RYŪ: TEN NO KATA

天之型

日撃 Nichigeki

1. The opponent's right hand grips my left lapel and his left hand grips the opening of my right sleeve at the elbow. I grasp the opponent's sleeve and lapel in the same manner.
2. The opponent attempts to throw me with Seoi-Nage, which I block by pushing my left hip against him as I pull my right elbow back.
3. I then strike to the opponent's face with the fingers of my right hand, turn to my left, step behind him with my right foot and throw him with Ōsoto-Nage.
4. Finally, I kick down to the opponent's right side with my right foot.

Ura Waza 1 (Variation 1): The same as the original technique, up until the strike to the opponent's face, after which I grasp his left lapel with my left hand and the palm of his right hand with my right. I then turn to my left, strike to the opponent's right armpit with my right hand and step backwards, to bring him down on his back.

Ura Waza 2 (Variation 2): The same as the previous variation, but without striking into the opponent's armpit, I step directly back with my left foot and drop to my left knee to bring the opponent down on his back. I finish by kicking to the opponent's right side with my right foot.

月肝 Gekkan

1. The opponent attacks with a straight right punch to the face.
2. I parry the attack with my left hand and grasp his wrist.
3. I then grasp the opponent's right shoulder with my right hand and pull, as I deliver a right kick to Suigetsu.
4. Finally, I step back with my right foot and drop to my right knee, bringing the opponent face down to the ground.

Ura Waza 1 (Variation 1): The same as the original technique, but after grasping the opponent's right wrist with my left hand, I wrap up his right arm with my right, place my right foot behind his and fall forwards, causing him to fall on his back. From this position, I apply a lock to his right arm.

Ura Waza 2 (Variation 2): The same as the original technique, but after grasping the opponent's right wrist with my left hand, I strike to Suigetsu with my right fist, wrap up his right arm from below with my right and throw him with Ippon-Seoi-Nage.

風靡 Fūbi

1. The opponent attacks with a double-lapel choke from the front.
2. I place my hands on the opponent's shoulders and jump up to scissor his torso with both my legs.
3. I strike to the opponent's face with my right hand, drop my shoulders back to the ground, grasp his ankles with both hands and pull, causing him to fall on his back.
4. I then roll backwards to a standing position.

Ura Waza 1 (Variation 1): The same as the original technique, but after wrapping my legs around the opponent's torso and striking to his face with my right hand, I drop my shoulders back to the ground and grasp his left ankle with my right hand and his right lapel with my left hand. I then push forwards with my legs, causing the opponent to fall on his back. As he falls,

I use my left-hand grip on his lapel to pull myself back up to a standing position above him.

Ura Waza 2 (Variation 2): The same as the original technique, but after wrapping my legs around the opponent's torso, I grasp both the opponent's lapels and pull to deliver a forehead strike to his face. I drop my shoulders back to the ground, bring both my hands down to his ankles and pull, causing him to fall on his back. I finally roll backwards to a standing position.

雨龍 Uryū

1. The opponent attempts to grab me from behind with Daki-Shime (bear hug).
2. I step forward with my left foot, shift my hips to my left and open my elbows to prevent the opponent from taking the hold.
3. I place my right thumb on the knuckles of the opponent's right hand as I grasp his palm with my other four fingers. I then lower my hips and lift my right hand to apply a lock on the opponent's wrist joint.
4. I step to my right with my left foot, while maintaining the lock on the opponent's wrist, and drop to my left knee to throw him with Katate-Nage.

Ura Waza 1 (Variation 1): The same as the original technique, except I grasp with my left hand, step to my left with my right foot and throw the opponent with a left-hand Katate-Nage.

Ura Waza 2 (Variation 2): The same as the original technique, except as I step to my right, I strike to the opponent's ribs with my left elbow, then throw him with Ippon-Seoi-Nage.

雲雀 Unjaku

1. The opponent attacks with a straight right punch to the face.
2. I drop down and touch the ground with both hands in front of the opponent, then strike up to his jaw from below with my right fist.
3. I grasp under the opponent's left armpit with my right hand and enter deeply with my right hip to throw him with Ganseki-Otoshi.

Ura Waza 1 (Variation 1): The same as the original technique but done on the left side.

Ura Waza 2 (Variation 2): The same as the original technique, except after grabbing the armpit with my right hand, I bring my right arm up to lock the opponent's left arm and throw him with Ganseki-Otoshi.

雪耀 Setsuyaku

1. The opponent attacks with a straight right punch to the face.
2. I parry the attack with my left arm and grasp his wrist.
3. I then wrap up the opponent's upper right arm from below with my right, to lock in such a way that if I apply force, it will break.
4. I grasp the opponent's right shoulder with my right hand, lower my hips and throw him with Ippon-Seoi-Nage.
5. Finally, I kick down to the opponent's right side with my right foot.

Ura Waza 1 (Variation 1): The same as the original technique but done on the left side with a left Ippon-Seoi-Nage.

Ura Waza 2 (Variation 2): The same as the original technique, except after I wrap up the opponent's upper right arm, I step in with my right foot to throw him with Ōsoto-Gake.

霧散 Musan

1. The opponent attacks with a straight right punch to the body.
2. I evade the attack by turning to my left and catching the opponent's wrist with my left hand.
3. I then strike to the opponent's face with my right fist and step under his right arm, twisting it into a lock.
4. Finally, I break the opponent's right elbow joint with a right-hand strike.

Ura Waza 1 (Variation 1): The same as the original technique but done on the left side.

Ura Waza 2 (Variation 2): The same as the original technique, except after I step under the opponent's right arm, I grasp his shoulder with my right hand, kick to the right side of his body with my right foot, step back and drop to my right knee, causing him to fall on his back.

霞雷 Karai

1. The opponent grabs my left lapel with his right hand.
2. I grasp his right wrist with my left hand, step back with my left foot and strike to his chest with a right punch.
3. I then grasp the opponent's shoulder with my right hand, take a big step back with my right foot and drop to my right knee, causing the opponent to fall face down.
4. I press down on the elbow joint of the opponent's right arm with my right shin, as my left hand lifts his wrist to apply a lock.

Ura Waza 1 (Variation 1): The same as the original technique but against a left grab.

Ura Waza 2 (Variation 2): The same as the original technique, except after I hold down the opponent with my right shin, I bring my left foot over the opponent to sit astride his back and apply Sankaku-Jime from behind.

5

SHINDEN FUDŌ RYŪ: CHI NO KATA

地之型

理拳 Riken

1. I am sitting in Fudōza with my left leg in front. The opponent is in Seiza, sitting on the points of his toes.
2. The opponent steps forward with his right foot and grabs my left lapel with his right hand. I grasp the opponent's right wrist with my right as my left leg kicks to the right side of his chest.
3. I then fall to my right side as I deliver a left-hand strike to the back of his right arm from above, causing him to fall face down.
4. Finally, I sit up and apply a lock to his right elbow joint.

Figure 2.5.1: Fudōza

Ura Waza 1 (Variation 1): The same as the original technique but I sit in Fudōza with my right leg in front for a left-side technique.

Ura Waza 2 (Variation 2): The same as the original technique, except after I kick, I then roll back to a standing position.

心拳 Shinken

1. I am sitting in Fudōza with my right leg in front. The opponent is in Seiza, sitting on the points of his toes.
2. The opponent steps forward with his right foot and grabs my left lapel with his right hand. I also step forward with my right foot to meet the opponent and grasp his lapels.
3. I strike with a right Shutō to Jakkotsu on the opponent's right arm, then kick to his jaw with my right foot as I roll backwards to a standing position.

Ura Waza 1 (Variation 1): The same as the original technique but I sit in Fudōza with my left leg in front for a left-side technique.

Ura Waza 2 (Variation 2): The same as the original technique, except as I roll back, I kick to the arm grasping my lapel to break the opponent's grip.

雷拳 Raiken

1. I am sitting in Fudōza with my right leg in front. The opponent is walking towards me.
2. The opponent attacks with a right kick, which I parry with my left arm to my left.
3. I then kick to the opponent's groin with my right foot to knock him down.

Ura Waza 1 (Variation 1): The same as the original technique but I sit in Fudōza with my left leg in front for a left-side technique.

Ura Waza 2 (Variation 2): The same as the original technique, except I kick to the opponent's right leg with my right foot to knock him down.

変虚 Henkyo

1. I sit facing the opponent in Fudōza.
2. The opponent stands up on his right leg, grabs my right lapel with his left hand and attacks with a right-handed stab, holding a Shōtō (short sword).
3. I cover the opponent's grabbing hand with my right and kick to Kinketsu the moment the Shōtō is thrust at me.
4. I then place my right thumb on the back of the opponent's left hand and turn to my right to apply Omote-Gyaku, causing him to fall on his back.
5. Finally, I kick to the left side of the opponent's chest with my right foot and step back.

Ura Waza 1 (Variation 1): The same as the original technique, except performed on the opposite side.

Ura Waza 2 (Variation 2): The same as the original technique, except instead of kicking to Kinketsu, I kick up under his jaw.

一閃 Issen

1. I am sitting in Fudōza with my right leg in front. The opponent is standing in front of me.
2. The opponent attacks with a right kick, which I parry with my left arm to my left.
3. The opponent then cuts down from above his head with a Shōtō. I parry the attack with my right hand and grasp his wrist.
4. I then sweep the opponent's left leg with my right foot, causing him to fall on his back.
5. Finally, I pin the opponent with Osaekomi (a hold down), twist the Shōtō from his grip and thrust it into his chest.

Ura Waza 1 (Variation 1): The same as the original technique, except performed on the opposite side.

Ura Waza 2 (Variation 2): The same as the original technique, except after I have swept the opponent's leg, I kick to his groin.

把拳 Akuken

1. I sit facing the opponent in Fudōza.
2. The opponent cuts down with a Daitō (long sword) from Daijōdan no Kamae.
3. I kick up at the opponent's hands as I roll backwards to a standing position.

Ura Waza 1 (Variation 1): The same as the original technique, except performed on the opposite side.

Ura Waza 2 (Variation 2): The same as the original technique, except after kicking up at the opponent's hands, I follow up by kicking to his groin.

乾抻 Kenkon

1. I am sitting in Fudōza. The opponent cuts down from behind me with a Daitō.
2. From a state of readiness, I evade the opponent's cut by placing my left hand on the ground to my left, so as the cut flows past my right side.
3. I rotate around, bringing my right leg to a standing position and taking the opponent's right arm in a lock by grasping his wrist with my left hand and wrapping up his right arm from below with my right.
4. I then tighten the lock on his arm, causing him to fall face-down.
5. Finally, I twist the sword from his grip with my left hand, step back and deliver a cut to his body.

Ura Waza 1 (Variation 1): The same as the original technique, except performed on the opposite side.

Ura Waza 2 (Variation 2): The same as the original technique, except after taking the sword, I step back into Kamae.

垂柳 **Suiryū**

1. I sit facing the opponent in Fudōza.
2. The opponent attacks with a straight thrust at my chest with a Daitō.
3. I evade by placing my right hand on the ground to my right, as my left hand grasps the opponent's right wrist.
4. I then capture his right arm from below with my right and kick to Suigetsu with my right foot.
5. Finally, I fall backwards with Te-Makura, while maintaining the lock on the opponent's arm and twist the sword from his grip.

Ura Waza 1 (Variation 1): The same as the original technique, except performed on the opposite side.

Ura Waza 2 (Variation 2): The same as the original technique, except after I grasp the opponent's wrist, I kick to Suigetsu.

6

SHINDEN FUDŌ RYŪ: SHIZEN SHIGOKU NO KATA

自然至極之型

體流 Tai-Nagashi

1. The opponent grabs my left lapel with his right hand. I grasp the opponent's right wrist with my left.
2. The opponent then attacks with a left punch to the face, which I parry with my right.
3. Next, I shift my weight to my right foot and grasp the opponent's left armpit with my right hand.
4. I slide my left foot in front of the opponent's left foot as I fall to my left side and pull strongly with my right hand, to throw the opponent over the top of me with Yoko-Nagare.

Ura Waza 1 (Variation 1): The same as the original technique, except performed on the opposite side.

Ura Waza 2 (Variation 2): The same as the original technique, except after throwing the opponent, I follow up with a strike to his left side.

拳流 Kobushi-Nagashi

1. The opponent grabs my right lapel with his left hand. I grasp the opponent's left wrist with my right, with my thumb pointing upwards.
2. The opponent then attacks with a right-hand strike to the left side of my head, which I parry with my left arm.
3. I bring my left hand down to grasp the opponent's right lapel, wrap up his left arm clockwise from above with my right and enter with my left hip to attempt a throw, which the opponent resists.
4. I then release my right arm and rotate my right hand anti-clockwise to capture the opponent's left elbow joint from below in Musō Dori.
5. I step back with my left leg and drop to my left knee, applying pressure to the opponent's left elbow joint and causing him to fall face-down.
6. Finally, I kick to the opponent's left side with my right foot.

Ura Waza 1 (Variation 1): The same as the original technique, except I complete the throw at Step 3.

Ura Waza 2 (Variation 2): The same as the original technique, except as I apply Musō Dori to his left arm, I turn to my left and kick up at his left leg with my right as I throw him with Uchi-Mata.

不抜 Fubatsu

1. The opponent grabs my right lapel with his left hand. I grasp the opponent's left shoulder with my right.
2. The opponent then attacks with a right-hand strike to the left side of my head which I parry with my left arm.
3. I kick to Suigetsu with my right foot and, in the same motion, pull my right foot diagonally back as I drop to my right knee and pull down with my right hand on the opponent's left shoulder to flip him over.

Ura Waza 1 (Variation 1): The same as the original technique, except I pull my right foot diagonally back and drop to my right knee without kicking first.

Ura Waza 2 (Variation 2): The same as the original technique, except as I pull my right foot diagonally back, I strike to the opponent's chest with my left elbow as I drop to my right knee to throw him.

両手掛 Ryote-Gake

1. The opponent attacks with a two-handed choke.
2. I grasp underneath the opponent's elbows with my hands and step back with my left foot.
3. As the opponent follows my movement, I raise his left elbow with my right hand and enter with my right hip to throw.

Ura Waza 1 (Variation 1): The same as the original technique, except as the opponent attacks with a choke, I kick to his groin with my right foot then enter with my right hip to throw.

Ura Waza 2 (Variation 2): The same as the original technique, except as the opponent attacks with a choke, I strike his ears with Happa-Ken, then thrust forward to knock him down in one movement.

鵲 Kasasagi

1. The opponent attacks with Hon-Jime.
2. I grasp underneath the opponent's elbows with my hands and throw him with Tomoe-Nage.

Ura Waza 1 (Variation 1): The same as the original technique, except as the opponent attacks with Hon-Jime, I throw the opponent with Yoko-Nagare to my left side.

Ura Waza 2 (Variation 2): The same as the original technique, except I throw the opponent with Yoko-Nagare to my right side.

鈴落 Suzu Otoshi

1. The opponent grabs my right lapel with his left hand. I lightly place my right hand just above the opponent's left elbow and grasp his left wrist with my left.
2. The opponent then strikes at my eyes with his right hand, which I parry with my left.
3. I then place my left hand on top of his right hand, take a step back with my left leg, drop to my left knee and hold the opponent face down as I apply a lock to his left elbow.

Ura Waza 1 (Variation 1): The same as the original technique, up to the opponent's strike with his right hand, where I kick to the opponent's groin with my right foot. I then hold the opponent face down as I apply a lock to his left elbow.

Ura Waza 2 (Variation 2): The same as the original technique, except I strike to the opponent's face with my left hand before placing it on top of the opponent's left hand. I then hold the opponent face down as I apply a lock to his left elbow.

霞落 Kasumi Otoshi

1. The opponent grabs my right lapel with his left hand, I place my right thumb on the back of it and keep my four fingers light, so they can grasp at any time.
2. The opponent then strikes at my eyes with his right hand.
3. I parry the attack with my left as my right hand grasps his left hand with my thumb on the back.
4. I turn to my left and apply Omote-Gyaku to throw the opponent.
5. Finally, I deliver a right kick to his side.

Ura Waza 1 (Variation 1): The same as the original technique, except after I parry the opponent's right-hand strike, I follow up with a left Shutō to the left side of his head. The remainder of the technique is the same.

Ura Waza 2 (Variation 2): The same as the original technique, except performed on the opposite side.

狼倒 **Rōto**

1. The opponent grasps my left lapel with his right hand, I place my right thumb on the back of it.
2. The opponent then attacks with a left punch. I temporarily release my right hand to parry the attack
3. I return my right thumb to the back of his right hand and apply Ura-Gyaku, as I deliver a left punch to the ribs on the right side of his body.
4. I step back with my right foot and drop to my right knee, bringing the opponent face-down to the ground.
5. Finally, I deliver a left kick to the opponent's right side.

Ura Waza 1 (Variation 1): The same as the original technique, except I deliver a left-hand strike to the opponent's face as I apply Ura-Gyaku.

Ura Waza 2 (Variation 2): The same as the original technique, except I kick to the opponent's groin as I apply Ura-Gyaku, then hold him down.

不動 **Fudō**

1. The opponent grabs my right lapel with his left hand. I lightly seize his grip from below with my right.
2. The opponent then attacks with a right punch. I parry with my left hand, then firmly grasp the palm area of his left hand with my right and lift it to lock the wrist joint in Omote-Take-Ori.
3. I then grasp the opponent's left shoulder with my left hand, turn to my left under his left arm, step back with my right foot and drop to my right knee, bringing the opponent down.

Ura Waza 1 (Variation 1): The same as the original technique, except after my left hand grasps his shoulder and I turn under his left arm, I then kick with my right foot into the calf of his left leg and pull him straight down in one movement.

Ura Waza 2 (Variation 2): The same as the original technique, except as the opponent's hand is taken in Take-Ori, I kick to his groin with my right foot, then thrust him straight down in one movement.

鶉刈 Ugari

1. The opponent grabs my left lapel with his right hand and my right sleeve with his left. I grasp the opponent's left armpit from below with my right.
2. The opponent throws me with Ōsoto-Nage.
3. I go with the throw and fall lightly to my right side, lying in front of the opponent's feet, as I pull firmly on the opponent's left armpit with my right hand.
4. The opponent is thrown sideways over the top of me.
5. I roll over to sit astride the opponent in Uma-Nori and apply Hon-Jime.

Ura Waza (Variation): The same as the original technique, except at the moment Ōsoto-Nage is applied, I grasp the opponent's right armpit with my left hand and strike in with my thumb. The rest of the technique remains the same.

不諱 Fukan

1. The opponent grabs my left lapel with his right hand and my right sleeve with his left. I remain in a natural posture with my arms relaxed and hanging naturally.
2. As the opponent attempts to throw me with Seoi-Nage, I strike to his face with my right hand as my left hand grasps the back of his belt and pulls.
3. I fall at his feet with Yoko-Nagare and the opponent is thrown over the top of me.

Ura Waza 1 (Variation 1): The same as the original technique, but instead of striking the face with my right hand, I strike to his right armpit.

Ura Waza 2 (Variation 2): The same as the original technique, except I strike strongly under the opponent's right elbow joint with my right fist.

自然 Shizen

1. The opponent grabs both my lapels. I remain in a natural posture.
2. As the opponent pulls strongly, I allow myself to be pulled forward and strike to his face with my forehead.
3. I then strike up under his chin with my right hand and throw him with Ōsoto-Nage.

Ura Waza 1 (Variation 1): The opponent grasps both my lapels. I remain in a natural posture. As the opponent pushes strongly, I allow myself to be pushed back as I grasp both his shoulders with my hands, kick up to his groin with my right foot and throw him with Tachi-Nagare.

Ura Waza 2 (Variation 2): If the opponent pushes, I use his pushing motion to punch to Suigetsu with my right fist. If he pulls, I use his pulling motion to kick up to his groin with my right foot. I always remain in a natural posture.

KUKISHIN RYŪ DAKENTAIJUTSU

九鬼神流打拳体術

7

KUKISHIN RYŪ: DAKENTAIJUTSU GOHŌ NO KAMAE

打拳体術五法之構

平之構 Hira no Kamae

I stand in a natural posture with both of my hands held in fists at my waist. I fix my eyes onto those of my opponent.

平一文字之構 Hira Ichimonji no Kamae

I stand with my feet apart and my arms extended out horizontally to either side in a straight line. The insides of my heels are in line with the outsides of my shoulders.

青眼之構 Seigan no Kamae

My left foot is facing forward in line with my left knee and my right foot is turned out and in line with my right knee. The insides of my heels are in line with the outsides of my shoulders. My left arm is extended forward, with my left hand open and pointed at the opponent. My right hand is held in a fist at my waist.

片手飛鳥之構 Katate Hichō no Kamae

My right foot is facing forward in line with my right knee and my left foot is turned out and pulled in behind my right foot. My hips are low. My right arm is extended forward, with my right hand open and pointed at the opponent. My left hand is held in a fist at chest height.

攻勢之構 Kōsei no Kamae

My right foot is pulled back half a step and my right and left feet are turned slightly out with my knees in line with them. My hips are low, and the insides of my heels are in line with the outsides of my shoulders. My left fist is held above my face and my right fist is held at chest height.

8

KUKISHIN RYŪ: SHODEN GATA
初伝型

生音 Seion

The opponent attacks by grabbing my left lapel with his right hand and my right sleeve with his left.

1. I match my opponent's grips by grasping his right sleeve under the elbow with my left hand and high on his left collar with my right.
2. In one movement, I pull with my left hand as I thrust forward with my right, to apply a collar choke.
3. I then raise my right foot out past the opponent's right leg and kick down to Kaku on the outside of his right knee.
4. I step back with my left foot and drop to my left knee, taking the opponent down to the ground in front of me.

鳥翼 Uyoku

The same as the previous technique up until I kick down to Kaku on the outside of the opponent's right knee, after which I turn in to throw him with Seoi-Nage.

夢落 Yume Otoshi

The opponent attacks with a left punch, right punch.

1. I parry the opponent's left punch with my right hand, his right punch with my left hand and grasp his sleeve.
2. I then press to Yūgasumi with my right hand as I take the opponent down with Ōsoto-Gake.

水翼 Suiyoku

The opponent attacks with a right punch, left punch, right kick.

1. I parry the opponent's right punch with my left hand, his left punch with my right hand and grasp the sleeve.
2. I then parry his right kick with my left hand, and in one motion, bring my left hand around to press Kirigasumi under the right side of his jaw.
3. Next, I kick to the opponent's lower left ankle with my right foot, pull his left sleeve with my right hand, step back with my right leg and drop to my right knee. As I do this, my left hand should be pushing hard on the point Kirigasumi to take the opponent down.

水車 Suisha

The opponent attacks with a right punch, left punch, right punch.

1. I strike up at opponent's right punch with my left hand, then punch to Sai on his inner left thigh with my right.
2. I parry his left punch with my right hand, his right punch with my left hand, grasp his right sleeve and pull.
3. Next, I grasp the tip of the opponent's left shoulder and pull with my right hand as I push with my left and kick up to Sai on his inner right thigh with my right foot.
4. I then wrap my right leg around his left leg and sweep it up to throw him diagonally to the right with Uchi-Mata.

首輪 **Kubiwa**

The opponent attacks with a right punch, left punch, right punch, left kick.

1. I parry the opponent's right punch with my left hand and his left punch with my right.
2. I parry his next right punch with my left, grasp the sleeve and pull.
3. I then parry the opponent's left kick with my right fist, striking to Sai on his inner left thigh.
4. I press down to the point Ryūmon with my right hand, pull hard on his right sleeve with my left, step back with my left foot and drop to my left knee to throw the opponent.

崩雪 **Hōsetsu**

The opponent attacks with a right punch, left punch, right kick, right punch.

1. I parry the opponent's right punch with my left hand and his left punch with my right.
2. I parry his right kick by striking to Sai on his inner right thigh with my right fist.
3. I parry his last right punch by knocking it down with my left hand.
4. Next, I grasp the opponent's left lapel from over his right arm with my left hand and a collar choke.
5. The opponent strikes up with his right hand from below my left arm to break my grip.
6. I change by turning to the outside of the opponent's right arm and throw him with Gyaku-Seoi-Nage.

磯嵐 **Iso Arashi**

The opponent grabs my right lapel with his left hand and attacks with a right punch, then a right kick.

1. I grasp the opponent's left wrist with my right hand and parry his right punch with my left.

2. I parry his right kick with my left hand.
3. I grasp the opponent's upper right lapel with my left hand and push up under the right side of his jaw.
4. I then apply Omote-Gyaku to his left wrist, step back with my right foot and drop to my right knee to throw the opponent.

柳折 Ryū Setsu

The opponent grabs my right lapel with his left hand and attacks with a right punch, then a right kick.

1. I lightly grasp the opponent's left hand holding my lapel in Omote-Gyaku and parry both the opponent's right punch and right kick with my left hand.
2. I then grasp the opponent's left elbow with my left hand and lift it upwards.
3. While holding the opponent's left hand in Omote-Gyaku, I turn my right foot sideways to kick to Sai on his inner left thigh, step back with my right foot and drop to my right knee to throw him.

吹雪 Fubuki

The opponent grabs my right lapel with his left hand and attacks with a right punch, then a right kick.

1. I lightly grasp the opponent's left hand holding my lapel in Omote-Gyaku and parry the opponent's right punch and right kick with my left hand.
2. I grasp the opponent's left elbow with my left hand, pull and lift it upwards.
3. I then kick up to the opponent's groin with my right foot, enter in with my left hip and throw him with Omote-Gyaku Seoi-Nage.

片帆 Kataho

The opponent attacks with a right punch, left punch, right kick, left kick, right punch.

1. I parry the opponent's right punch with my left hand and his left punch with my right.

2. I parry the opponent's right kick by striking to Sai on his inner right thigh with my left fist, then his left kick by striking Sai on his inner left thigh with my right fist.
3. I catch his last right punch with Jūmonji-Uke.
4. I apply Ura-Oni-Kudaki to the opponent's right arm as I throw him with Ōsoto-Nage.

竜巻 Tatsumaki

The opponent attacks with a right punch, left punch, right kick, left kick, right punch.

1. I parry the opponent's right punch with my left hand and his left punch with my right.
2. I parry the opponent's right kick by striking to Kaku on the inside of his right knee joint with my right fist, then his left kick by striking to Kaku on the inside of his left knee joint with my left fist.
3. I catch the opponent's last right punch with Jūmonji-Uke, grasp his right sleeve with my left hand and pull.
4. The opponent attacks with a left punch.
5. I strike up with my right fist to Hoshi-Shita on the inside of his left arm, then push strongly with my right hand to Amado on the left side of his neck.
6. I kick with my right heel to Kaku on the opponent's right leg, pull hard on his right sleeve with my left hand and throw him with Ōsoto-Nage.

9

KUKISHIN RYŪ: CHŪDEN GATA
中伝型

浦波 Ura Nami

The opponent attacks with a right punch, left punch, right kick, right punch.

1. I parry the opponent's right punch with my left hand and his left punch with my right.
2. I parry the opponent's right kick with my left hand by striking to Kaku.
3. I parry his last right punch with my left hand, bring my right hand over his right arm and apply Ura-Oni-Kudaki.
4. I then kick to Kaku on the inside of the opponent's right leg with my right foot, tighten the Oni-Kudaki lock on his right arm and bring my right foot down strongly to throw him with Ōsoto-Nage.

天地 Tenchi

The opponent attacks with a right punch, left punch, right punch, right kick, right punch.

1. I parry the opponent's right punch with my left hand, his left punch with my right, kick his next right punch up to the left and

his right kick with my left hand by striking to Sai on the outside of his right leg.

2. I catch the opponent's last right punch by crossing my wrists for Jūmonji-Uke.
3. I then grasp the point Hoshi-Shita on the opponent's right arm with my right and pull.
4. I grasp the outside of the opponent's right hand with my left and apply Omote-Gyaku.
5. I kick up to Suzu with my right shin, step back with my left foot, drop to my left knee and apply downward pressure to the lock on the opponent's right hand to take him down.

方波 Kata Nami

The opponent attacks with a right punch, right kick, right punch.

1. Against the opponent's right punch, I strike up at Hoshi-Shita on his right arm with my left fist. Against his right kick, I strike to Sai on his right leg with my right fist.
2. I parry his last right punch with my left hand and grasp his sleeve.
3. I then strike to Kirigasumi with my right thumb, step to the opponent's right side and throw him with Harai-Goshi.

霞掛 Kasumi Gake

The opponent attacks with a right punch, right kick, right punch.

1. Against the opponent's right punch, I strike up at Hoshi-Shita on his right arm with my left fist. Against his right kick, I strike to Sai on his right leg with my right fist.
2. I then strike to the opponent's forehead with my right hand.
3. I parry the opponent's last right punch with my left arm, grasp his sleeve and pull down.
4. I next grasp the point Hoshi-Shita on the opponent's right arm with my right hand and pull down again.
5. I then utilise the opponent's reaction to change and throw him with Ippon-Seoi-Nage.

瀧之瀬 Taki no Se

The opponent attacks with a right punch, right kick, right punch.

1. Against the opponent's right punch, I strike up at Hoshi-Shita on his right arm with my left fist. Against his right kick, I strike to Sai on his right leg with my right fist. I parry the opponent's last right punch with my left hand.
2. The opponent then takes my left wrist with his right hand and enters in to attack with Hane-Goshi-Nage using his right leg.
3. I strike strongly to the point Sai on the opponent's right leg with my right hand to sweep it away.
4. I grasp his right shoulder with my left hand, grasp his left wrist with my right and press down with my left arm.
5. I then utilise the opponent's reaction to change and enter with my left hip to throw him.

塩風 Shio Kaze

The opponent attacks with a right punch, right kick, right punch.

1. Against the opponent's right punch, I strike up at Hoshi-Shita on his right arm with my left fist. Against his right kick, I strike to Sai on his right leg with my right fist. I parry the opponent's last right punch with my left hand, grasp his right sleeve and kick up to Kaku on the inside of his left leg with my right foot.
2. I then grasp the opponent's right hand in Ura-Gyaku with my left hand and Hoshi-Shita on the opponent's right arm with my right.
3. I step back with my left foot and drop to my left knee to throw the opponent.

山嵐 Yama Arashi

The opponent grasps my right lapel with his left hand and punches with his right.

1. I step back with my right foot and parry his right punch with my left arm.
2. I then apply Omote-Gyaku with my right hand on the opponent's

left, turn to step back with my right foot and throw him with
Ippon Seoi-Nage.

柳風 Yanagi Kaze

The opponent grabs my right lapel with his left hand and punches with
his right.

1. I step back with my right foot and parry with my left arm.
2. I then apply Take-Ori with my right hand to the opponent's left,
   rotate clockwise under his right arm to apply torsion, kick to Yaku
   on his left leg with my left foot and pull him down.

龍波 Tatsu Nami

The opponent grabs my right lapel with his left hand and punches with
his right.

1. I parry the opponent's right punch with my left hand then grasp
   his left sleeve at his elbow from above with my left hand.
2. I strike to Butsumetsu on the left side of the opponent's body
   with my right hand and grasp under his left armpit.
3. I apply a lock to the opponent's left arm as I step back with my
   left foot and drop my left knee to the ground to pull him down.
4. I hold the opponent down (Osaekomi).

虎尾 Ko-o

The opponent grabs my right lapel with his left hand and punches with
his right.

1. I parry the opponent's right punch with my left hand.
2. I take the opponent's left wrist in Omote-Gyaku with my right as I
   grasp the point Hoshi-Shita on his right arm with my left hand
   and pull.
3. I then step between the opponent's legs with my right foot and
   wrap up his left leg from the inside for Ō-Uchi-Gake as I strike up
   to Asagasumi with my right hand to thrust him straight down on
   his back.

重岩 Kasane Iwa

The opponent grabs my right lapel with his left hand and punches with his right.

1. I parry the opponent's right punch with my left hand.
2. I grasp the opponent's left lapel with my right hand and his left elbow from above with my left.
3. I then pull in with my left hand to catch his left wrist against my chest in Take-Ori.
4. Finally, I step in with my left leg to take the opponent down with Ōsoto-Gake.

四方捕 Shihō Dori

The opponent grabs my lapel with his left hand and punches with his right.

1. I step back with my right foot, parry the opponent's right punch with my left hand and grasp his wrist.
2. I then bring my right hand up from below his right arm, clasp my hands together and apply Omote-Oni-Kudaki.
3. Next, I step back with my right foot, enter with my left hip and throw the opponent with Gyaku-Seoi-Nage.

10

KUKISHIN RYŪ: SABAKI GATA
捌型

荒駒 Arakoma

The opponent grabs my lapel with his left hand and attacks with a right kick then a right punch.

1. I lightly hold the opponent's left hand in Ura-Gyaku with my right hand and parry his right kick and punch with my left.
2. I strike to Asagasumi with my left hand, then throw the opponent with a dropping Koshi-Nage.

鹿足 Kasoku

The opponent grabs my lapel with his left hand and attacks with a right kick then a right punch.

1. I lightly hold the opponent's left hand in Ura-Gyaku with my right hand and parry his right kick and punch with my left.
2. I kick to the point Kaku on the inside of the opponent's right leg with the sole of my right foot.
3. I then wrap up the opponent's left ankle from the inside with my left foot, strike to Kimon with my left hand, apply Ura-Gyaku to his left hand with my right and take him down with Ko-Uchi-Gake.

竹声 Chikusei

The opponent attacks with a right punch, left punch, right kick, right punch.

1. I parry the opponent's right punch with my left hand, his left punch with my right, grasp his sleeve and pull.
2. I parry his right kick with my left leg.
3. I parry his last right punch and grasp his right wrist with my left hand.
4. I then grab the opponent's ribs under his right arm with my right hand and pull to my left.
5. Finally, I strike to Butsumetsu on the opponent's lower chest area with my right hand and throw him with a right Harai-Goshi.

夢枕 Yume Makura

The opponent attacks with a right punch, left punch, right kick, right punch.

1. I parry the opponent's right punch with my left hand, his left punch with my right hand and his right kick by punching to Sai on his right leg with my right fist.
2. I catch the opponent's last right punch by crossing my wrists for Jūmonji-Uke, grasp his right sleeve with my right hand and pull.
3. I lock the opponent's right hand in Ura-Gyaku with my left, then enter as if to throw with Ippon-Seoi-Nage, but instead turn back to throw him with Te-Makura.

裾捌 Suso Sabaki

The opponent attacks with a right punch, left punch, right kick, right punch.

1. I parry the opponent's right punch with my left hand, his left punch with my right hand and his right kick by punching to Sai on his right leg with my right fist.
2. I parry the opponent's last right punch by striking up to Hoshi-Shita on his right arm with my left, then step to my right and grasp his left sleeve with my left hand.

3. I take the opponent's left wrist in Ura-Gyaku with my right hand, grab his left armpit with my left, enter with my left hip to set up for Koshi-Nage.
4. I utilise his reaction and change by stepping back with my right foot and dropping to my right knee to throw him.

磯返 Iso Gaeshi

The opponent attacks with a right punch, left punch, right kick, right punch.

1. I parry the opponent's right punch with my left hand, his left punch with my right hand and his right kick by punching to Sai on his right leg with my right fist.
2. I parry the opponent's last right punch with my left hand, take his right hand in Ura-Gyaku with my right, turn my hips to the outside and throw him with Katate-Nage.

風払 Kaze Harai

The opponent grabs my lapel with his left hand and attacks with a right punch, then a right kick.

1. First, I strike up to Hoshi-Shita on the opponent's left arm as he grabs and grasp hold.
2. I then parry the opponent's right punch by striking to Hoshi-Shita on his right arm with my left hand and his right kick by striking to Sai on his right leg with my left hand.
3. I control the opponent's left hand with my right in Ura-Gyaku, step back with my left foot and lift the opponent's right hand high to tighten the lock.
4. I then step under the opponent's left arm and turn to apply pressure to the lock and flip the opponent on his back.

車捕 Kuruma Dori

The opponent grabs my lapel with his left hand and attacks with a right punch, then a right kick.

1. First, I strike up to the point Hoshi-Shita on the opponent's left arm that is holding my lapel and grab hold.
2. I then parry the opponent's right punch by striking to the point Hoshi-Shita on his right arm with my left hand and parry his right kick by punching to the point Sai on his right leg with my left hand.
3. Next, I take the opponent's left hand in a lock with Ura-Gyaku with my right, step back with my left foot and lift the opponent's right hand high to tighten the lock.
4. I enter with my hips to throw him with Koshi-Nage.

鬼門 Kimon

The opponent attacks with a right punch, left punch, right kick, left kick, left punch.

1. I parry the opponent's right punch with my left hand, his left punch with my right hand, parry his right kick by striking with my right fist to sweep it away and parry his left kick by striking with my left fist to sweep that away too.
2. I parry the opponent's last left punch with my right hand, grasp his sleeve, then wind up his left arm from the inside with my right.
3. I take a step back with my left foot and drop to my left knee to throw the opponent with Katate-Nage.

裏鬼門 Ura Kimon

The opponent attacks with a right punch, left punch, right kick, left kick, right punch.

1. I parry the opponent's right punch with my left hand, his left punch with my right hand, parry his right kick by striking with my right fist to sweep it away and parry his left kick by striking with my left fist to sweep that away too.

2. I catch the opponent's last right punch with Jūmonji-Uke.
3. I grasp the opponent's right wrist with my left hand from the outside, then roll my left hand around to wind up his right arm from the inside and grasp his sleeve to apply a lock.
4. I kick up to Suzu with my right foot then throw the opponent with Ōsoto-Gake.

浮藻 **Ukimo**

The opponent attacks with a right punch, left punch, right kick, left kick then right punch.

1. I parry the opponent's right punch with my left hand, his left punch with my right hand, parry his right kick by striking with my right fist to sweep it away and parry his left kick by striking with my left fist to sweep that away too.
2. I catch the opponent's last right punch with Jūmonji-Uke.
3. I grasp the opponent's right wrist with my left hand from the outside, then roll my left hand around to wind up his right arm from the inside and grasp his sleeve to apply a lock.
4. I kick up to Suzu with my right foot then throw the opponent with Ippon-Seoi-Nage.

乱風 **Ranfū**

The opponent attacks with a right punch, left punch, right kick, left kick then right punch.

1. I parry the opponent's right punch with my left hand, his left punch with my right hand, parry his right kick by striking with my right fist to sweep it away and parry his left kick by striking with my left fist to sweep that away too.
2. I catch the opponent's last right punch with Jūmonji-Uke.
3. I grasp the opponent's right wrist with my left hand from the outside, then roll my left hand around to wind up his right arm from the inside and grasp his sleeve to apply a lock.
4. I kick up to Suzu with my right foot then drop to my right knee and throw the opponent with Ippon-Seoi-Nage.

11

KUKISHIN RYŪ: OKUDEN GATA
奥伝型

風雲 Fūun

The opponent attacks with a right punch, left punch, right kick, left kick, right punch.

1. I parry the opponent's right punch with my left hand, his left punch with my right hand, his right kick by striking to Sai with my left hand and his left kick by also striking to Sai with my left hand.
2. I catch the opponent's last right punch with Jūmonji-Uke and apply Oni-Kudaki.
3. After breaking the opponent's right arm, I then step under his arm to come out the right side, kick to Sai on the opponent's right leg with my left foot and pull, so as the opponent falls face down.

扠技 Sagi

The opponent attacks with a right punch, left punch, right kick, left kick, right punch.

1. I parry the opponent's right punch with my left hand, his left punch with my right hand, his right kick by striking to Sai with

my left hand and his left kick by also striking to Sai with my left hand.
2. I catch the opponent's last right punch with Jūmonji-Uke and apply Oni-Kudaki.
3. I kick up to Suzu with a right shin kick.
4. I then drop to my knee to throw the opponent with Ippon-Seoi-Nage.

返技 Kaeshi Waza

The opponent attacks with a right punch, left punch, right kick, left kick, right punch.

1. I parry the opponent's right punch with my left hand, his left punch with my right hand, his right kick by striking to Sai with my left hand and his left kick by also striking to Sai with my left hand.
2. I catch the opponent's last right punch with Jūmonji-Uke, then grasp Hoshi-Shita at his right elbow joint with my right hand.
3. I bring my left hand over the opponent's right arm and apply Musha-Dori.
4. I kick to Suigetsu with my right foot, take a large step back with my left foot and drop to my left knee so as the opponent falls on his back.

鬼落 Oni Otoshi

The opponent attacks with a right punch, left punch, right kick, left kick, right punch.

1. I parry the opponent's right punch with my left hand, parry his left punch with my right hand, parry his right kick by striking to the point Sai with my left hand and parry his left kick by also striking to the point Sai with my left hand.
2. I catch the opponent's last right punch with Jūmonji-Uke, then grasp Hoshi-Shita at his right elbow joint with my right hand.
3. I bring my left hand over the opponent's right arm and apply Musha-Dori.
4. I kick up to Suzu with a right shin kick then take the opponent down with Ōsoto-Gake.

岩砕 Iwa Kudaki

The opponent attacks freely with right and left punches and right and left kicks. I parry his punches by striking to the points Hoshi-Shita or Kyohaku and parry his kicks by striking to Sai on the inside of his thighs.

1. I parry the opponent's last right punch from the inside with my left hand.
2. I then strike with a right Chin-Ken to either the opponent's sternum, face or eyes.
3. I throw the opponent with Harai-Goshi.

Figure 2.11.1: Chin-Ken

雪倒 Yuki Taoshi

The opponent attacks freely with right and left punches and right and left kicks. I parry his punches by striking to the points Hoshi-Shita or Kyohaku and parry his kicks by striking to Sai on the inside of his thighs.

1. I parry the opponent's last right punch with my right hand by punching up to Hoshi-Shita on the opponent's right arm.
2. I take the opponent's right hand with my left in Ura-Gyaku, grasp his left shoulder with my right hand and kick to Suzu with my left shin.
3. I then take a big step back with my right foot and drop to my right knee, bringing the opponent face down to the ground.

剛倒 **Gō Taoshi**

The opponent attacks freely with right and left punches and right and left kicks. I parry his punches by striking to the points Hoshi-Shita or Kyohaku and parry his kicks by striking to Sai on the inside of his thighs.

1. I parry the opponent's last right punch with my right hand by punching up to Hoshi-Shita on the opponent's right arm.
2. I then take the opponent's right hand with my left in Ura-Gyaku and throw him with Hane-Goshi-Nage.

挐風 **Dofū**

The opponent attacks freely with right and left punches and right and left kicks. I parry his punches by striking to the points Hoshi-Shita or Kyohaku and parry his kicks by striking to Sai on the inside of his thighs.

1. I parry the opponent's last right punch with my left arm and take his wrist in Ura-Gyaku.
2. I then strike to Kasumi on the left side of the opponent's head with a right Shutō, catch his left leg from the inside with my right foot and take him down backward with Ō-Uchi-Gake.

鬼砕 **Oni Kudaki**

The opponent attacks freely with right and left punches and right and left kicks. I parry his punches by striking to the points Hoshi-Shita or Kyohaku and parry his kicks by striking to Sai on the inside of his thighs.

1. I catch the opponent's last right punch with Jūmonji-Uke.
2. I then grasp the opponent's right sleeve with my right hand and pull as I kick to Suzu with my right foot.
3. Finally, I scoop up the opponent's right arm with my left hand from the outside and throw him with Gyaku-Seoi-Nage.

柳風 **Yanagi Kaze**

The opponent attacks freely with right and left punches and right and left kicks. I parry his punches by striking to the points Hoshi-Shita or Kyohaku and parry his kicks by striking to Sai on the inside of his thighs.

1. I parry the opponent's last right punch with my left hand.
2. The opponent then grabs my left hand with his right, my left shoulder with his left and attempts to throw me with Harai-Goshi.
3. I lower my hips to block the throw, strike with my right thumb to Koe, at the indentation of his hip joint, strike to Kimon with my left elbow and slide my left foot behind the opponent on his right side to throw him with Yoko-Nagare.

太刀打 Tachi Uchi

The opponent attacks freely with right and left punches and right and left kicks. I parry his punches by striking to the points Hoshi-Shita or Kyohaku and parry his kicks by striking to Sai on the inside of his thighs.

1. The opponent then attempts to throw me with Koshi-Nage.
2. I lower my hips to block the throw, grasp Butsumetsu on each side, under the opponent's arms from behind, press down, then turn to throw him with Gyaku-Koshi-Nage (Ōsoto-Nage).

撥倒 Hane Taoshi

The opponent attacks freely with right and left punches and right and left kicks. I parry his punches by striking to the points Hoshi-Shita or Kyohaku and parry his kicks by striking to Sai on the inside of his thighs.

1. The opponent then attempts to throw me with Hane-Goshi-Nage. I lower my hips to block the throw.
2. As the opponent steps back to his original position, I enter in with my hips, press to Amado and throw the opponent with Koshi-Nage.

12

KUKISHIN RYŪ: SHIRABE MOGURI GATA
調潜型

潜捕 **Moguri Dori**

The opponent attacks, striking freely.

1. I parry the opponent's punches by striking to Hoshi-Shita or Jakkotsu and parry his kicks by striking to Sai, Yaku or Kaku.
2. When I see a chance, I step back to Seigan no Kamae, Kōsei no Kamae or Katate Hichō no Kamae to draw in the opponent's attack.
3. If after I parry his punch, I am then unable to grasp his sleeve or wrist, I withdraw another step and try to draw him in again.
4. Once I grasp the opponent's wrist or sleeve, I strike to Ryūmon, Amado or any other easy target with my right hand, then enter with my left hip to throw him. If I strike with my left hand, I enter with my right hip to throw.

車輪 **Sharin**

The opponent attacks, striking freely.

1. I parry the opponent's last right punch with my left hand.
2. The opponent then grabs my left hand and attempts to throw me with Harai-Goshi.

3. I lower my hips to block the throw, thrust up at Amado from behind with my right hand and press to the point Koe at his hip with my left.
4. I then pull back and drop to my left knee to pull the opponent down on his back (Otoshi-Nage).

虎伏 Torafushi

The opponent attacks, striking freely.

1. I catch the opponent's last right punch with Jūmonji-Uke, then grasp the opponent's right sleeve with my right hand and apply Ura-Gyaku with my left.
2. Next, I strike to Asagasumi with my right hand, grasp the point of his chin, kick to Suzu with my right foot and step in for Ōsoto-Gake.
3. From the Ōsoto-Gake position, I drop to my left knee to bring the opponent straight down on his back (Ōsoto Kuzushi).

龍伏 Ryūfuku

The opponent attacks, striking freely.

1. On the opponent's last right punch, I grasp his right lapel with my left hand.
2. The opponent then steps in, attempting to throw me with Seoi-Nage.
3. I lower my hips to block the throw, then press to Koe on his hip with my right hand.
4. The opponent steps back to withdraw to his original position.
5. I follow and strike to Amado with my right hand, catch the inside of the opponent's left thigh with my right foot and take him down with Ō-Uchi-Gake.
6. As I execute the throw, I grasp the opponent's left shoulder with my right hand and pull as I strike to Amado with my left hand.

飛違 Tobi Chigai

The opponent attacks, striking freely.

1. I parry the opponent's last right punch with my left hand, grasp his sleeve and pull.
2. The opponent then attacks with Koshi-Nage.
3. I push to Butsumetsu on the opponent's right side with my right hand.
4. The opponent steps back to withdraw to his original position and attacks again with Ōsoto-Nage.
5. I strike to Amado with my right hand, then push up at the point of his chin with the same right hand.
6. Finally, I use the opponent's right arm to throw him with Ippon-Seoi-Nage.

山落 Yama Otoshi

The opponent attacks, striking freely.

1. I parry the opponent's last right punch with my left hand and grasp his sleeve.
2. The opponent grabs my left wrist with his right hand, my right lapel with his left and attempts to throw me with Harai-Goshi.
3. I lower my hips to block the throw, then strike to Kasumi with the four fingers of my right hand (Shishi-Suiken), then to Jinchū with my right thumb.
4. The opponent steps back to withdraw to his original position.
5. I grasp the opponent's right hand with my left in Ura-Gyaku, enter with my hip and throw him.

擲落 Teki Otoshi

The opponent attacks, striking freely.

1. I parry the opponent's last right punch with my left hand by striking to Hoshi-Shita on his right elbow joint, grasp his sleeve and pull.
2. The opponent then punches with his left hand, which I parry with my right, grasp his sleeve and push upward.

3. I then kick to the point Sai with my right foot and drop to my right knee while pulling down to throw the opponent.

敵当 Heitō

The opponent attacks, striking freely.

1. I parry the opponent's last right punch with my left hand, grasp his sleeve and pull.
2. The opponent then grabs my lapel while entering to throw me with Harai-Goshi. I lower my hips to block the throw.
3. The opponent returns to his original position. I enter in, sweep his right hand up with my left hand and push up to Asagasumi with my right.
4. I then take the opponent's right hand with my left in Omote-Gyaku and strike to Butsumetsu with my right hand to knock him down.

鼯 Musasabi

The opponent attacks, striking freely.

1. I parry the opponent's last right punch with my left hand, grasp his sleeve and pull him in while thrusting my right hand into his left armpit.
2. The opponent then attempts to throw me with Koshi-Nage.
3. I lower my hips to block the throw and press to Koe on the opponent's hip with my right hand.
4. The opponent steps back to withdraw to his original position.
5. I take the opponent's right wrist in Ura-Gyaku, kick up to his groin with my right foot, wrap up his right leg with my right, then throw him with a right side Harai-Goshi.

玉投 Tama Nage

The opponent attacks, striking freely.

1. I parry the opponent's last right punch with my left hand, grasp his sleeve and pull him in while thrusting my right hand into his left armpit.

2. The opponent then attempts to throw me with Keri-Goshi (Kicking Hip Throw).
3. I lower my hips to block the throw and press to Koe on the opponent's hip with my right hand.
4. The opponent steps back to withdraw to his original position.
5. I take the opponent's right wrist in either Omote or Ura Gyaku, grasp his right elbow with my left hand, step back with my right foot and press down.
6. I then turn back, push up to the underside of the opponent's chin and throw him with Harai-Goshi.

投逆 Gyaku Nage

The opponent attacks, striking freely.

1. I parry the opponent's last right punch with my left hand, place my right hand to Asagasumi and attempt to throw him with Uchi-Mata.
2. The opponent evades the throw and punches with his left hand.
3. I parry with my right, grab his sleeve and attempt to strike to his face with my fingers held in Chin-Ken.
4. The opponent blocks my strike.
5. I take the opponent's left hand in Ura-Gyaku with my right.
6. I then place my right hand to Asagasumi and throw him with Ōsoto-Nage.

打払 Uchiharai

The opponent attacks, striking freely.

1. I parry the opponent's right punch with my left hand, then use the same left hand to strike at his face with Chin-Ken.
2. The opponent evades my strike and attacks with a left punch.
3. I parry the opponent's left punch with my right hand, then use the same right hand to strike at his face with Chin-Ken
4. The opponent evades my strike once again.
5. I kick with my right foot, which is parried by the opponent.
6. I take a step back, the opponent steps forward to attack with a right punch.

7. I lower my hips and parry with my left hand, then use the same left hand to strike to his face with Chin-Ken.
8. I then strike to Suigetsu with my right hand.
9. Finally, I leap in, bring my right arm up high from behind his left arm, enter with my hips and throw him with Gyaku-Seoi-Nage.

TAKAGI YOSHIN RYŪ JŪTAIJUTSU

高木揚心流柔体術

13

TAKAGI YOSHIN RYŪ: SHODEN OMOTE GATA
初伝表型

霞捕 **Kasumi Dori**

Suwari-Waza (Seated Technique).

1. The opponent and I face each other in Seiza, sitting on the points of our toes. The opponent steps forward with his right foot and grabs my left lapel with his right hand. I grasp my own left lapel with my left hand, controlling the opponent's grip from below.
2. I then stand up with my right foot and strike to Kasumi on the right side of the opponent's head with a right Ura-Shutō.
3. Next, I grasp the opponent's right lapel with my right hand, step back in a big motion with my right foot and place my right knee down behind me to bring the opponent face down to the floor.
4. Finally, I kick to the opponent's chest with my left foot and hold him down.

洞返 **Dō Gaeshi**

Suwari-Waza (Seated Technique).

1. The opponent attacks with a right punch to Suigetsu.
2. I parry the attack from the outside with my right hand and grasp his wrist.

3. I grasp the opponent's left collar from the front with my left hand, then step out to the side with my left foot and pull to drop the opponent onto his back.
4. Next, I apply pressure to the back of the opponent's right elbow with my left leg to turn him over onto his front.
5. I hold him down as my left hand applies a collar choke.

搦捕 Karame Dori

Tachi-Waza (Standing Technique).

1. The opponent is walking forwards. I follow behind him.
2. I grasp the opponent's collar from behind his neck with my right hand. As he tries to turn around, I kick to his Achilles with my right foot and pull him down to the floor.

虚倒 Kyotō

Suwari-Waza (Seated Technique).

1. From standing, the opponent attacks with a right kick to Suigetsu.
2. I evade diagonally back as I parry the kick with my right hand and grasp his ankle at the Achilles.
3. I then feed my left hand between my right arm and the opponent's right shin, roll my hand over and apply a lock to his ankle.
4. I stand up and pull so that the opponent falls face down.
5. Finally, I strike to the opponent's Achilles with a right Shutō and withdraw.

片胸捕 Katamune Dori

Tachi-Waza (Standing Technique).

1. The opponent grabs my left lapel with his right hand. I grasp my own left lapel with my left hand, controlling the opponent's grip from below.
2. I strike to Kasumi on the right side of the opponent's head with a right Ura-Shutō, then place my right thumb on the back of his right hand with my four fingers grasping his palm.
3. I step back with my left leg, break the opponent's grip on my

lapel, kick to his inner right thigh with my left foot, step back and pull so that the opponent falls face down.

4. I then hold the opponent down by applying pressure to his right shoulder with my left hand, as I lift his right wrist up high with my right to apply Ō-Gyaku.

両胸捕 **Ryōmune Dori**

Tachi-Waza (Standing Technique).

1. The opponent grabs my lapels with both hands. I grasp my own lapels, controlling the opponent's grips from below.
2. I strike to the opponent's face with the palm of my right hand from between his arms.
3. I then place my right thumb on the back of his right hand with my four fingers grasping his palm.
4. I step back with my left leg and break the opponent's right grip on my lapel, kick to the opponent's inner right thigh with my left foot, step back and pull, so that the opponent falls face down.
5. I then hold the opponent down by applying pressure to his right shoulder with my left hand, as I lift his right wrist up high with my right to apply Ō-Gyaku.

追掛捕 **Oikake Dori**

Tachi-Waza (Standing Technique).

1. The opponent is walking forwards. I follow behind him.
2. From close behind, I give a Kiai (a shout), causing the opponent to attempt to turn around to face me.
3. I strike with a right Ura-Shutō to Kasumi on the right side of his head, scoop up with my right arm from below his right shoulder, wrap up his right leg with my right and throw him so as he lands on his back.
4. I then hold the opponent down by applying a lock to his right arm.

戒後砕 **Kaigo Kudaki**

Tachi-Waza (Standing Technique).

1. The opponent attempts to apply Hagai-Jime (full nelson) from behind me.
2. I spread my arms out and turn my hips to my left to prevent the opponent from taking the hold.
3. I then rotate my right arm and shoulder underneath the opponent's right arm, grasp his right wrist with my right hand, turn my hips in, drop to my right knee and throw him in a similar style to Seoi-Nage (my right shoulder under his right armpit and both hands grasping his right wrist).

行違 **Iki Chigai**

Tachi-Waza (Standing Technique).

1. The opponent and I approach each other, passing by our right sides.
2. As I pass the opponent, I catch his right wrist with my right hand, lift it up and strike with my left elbow to the ribs under his right arm.
3. I then pull his arm back as I scoop up his right ankle with my right ankle so that he falls onto his back.
4. While still holding the opponent's wrist, I kick to his right side with my right foot.

唯逆 **Yuigyaku**

Tachi-Waza (Standing Technique).

1. The opponent and I approach each other.
2. The opponent attacks with a right punch to the left side of my face.
3. I parry the attack with my left arm, deliver a right punch to his face, then follow up by wrapping up his left leg with my right for Ō-Uchi-Gake, causing the opponent to fall on his back.
4. I hold him down by applying Ryō-Gokansetsu-Tori (a lock to both

hip joints by applying pressure to the insides of his thighs with my knees).

乱勝 Ranshō

Tachi-Waza (Standing Technique).

1. The opponent attacks with a right punch.
2. I step diagonally back with my right foot and parry the attack with my left arm.
3. I then strike up with my right hand to Asagasumi and wrap up the opponent's right leg from the outside with my left for Ko-Soto-Gake, causing the opponent to fall on his back.

拳流 Ken Nagare

Tachi-Waza (Standing Technique).

1. The opponent attacks with a right punch to Suigetsu.
2. I take a small step forward with my left foot and turn to evade the punch to the outside as I grasp his wrist with my right hand.
3. I then step back with my right foot and pull with my right hand as I drop to my right knee, causing the opponent to fall face down.
4. Finally, I hold the opponent down by applying pressure to the back of his right elbow with my left hand and deliver a left toe-kick to his right side.

膝車 Hiza Guruma

Tachi-Waza (Standing Technique).

1. The opponent is sitting in Seiza.
2. I step in and deliver a kick at the seated opponent, which he blocks with his right hand.
3. I grasp his right wrist as he blocks my kick and step to my right to bring him face down to the floor.
4. Finally, I lift, twist and press down on his right arm to hold him down.

14

TAKAGI YOSHIN RYŪ: ERI JIME GATA

襟締型

本締 Hon-Jime

Tachi-Waza (Standing Technique).

1. I grasp the opponent's lower left lapel with my left hand and his upper right lapel with my right. My right thumb is on the inside of his collar.
2. I pull with my left hand and turn my right wrist, in an action similar to opening a jar, to apply pressure to the artery on the right side of his neck.

逆締 Gyaku-Jime

Tachi-Waza (Standing Technique).

1. I grasp the opponent's lower left lapel with my left hand and his upper right lapel with my right. My right thumb is on the outside and my fingers are on the inside of his collar.
2. I pull with my left hand and turn my right wrist to apply pressure to the artery on the right side of his neck with my fingers.

腕締 Ude-Jime

Tachi-Waza (Standing Technique).

1. The opponent grabs my left lapel with his right hand.
2. I grasp the opponent's right wrist with my left hand and bring my right hand up from under his right arm to grasp my left lapel above his gripping hand.
3. I then place my right foot outside the opponent's right foot and fall forwards to drop him on his back.
4. I press down on the opponent's right wrist with my left hand to hold it down and apply an armlock by pushing his arm up towards his head.

一摘締 Itteki-Jime

Tachi-Waza (Standing Technique).

1. I take a high grip on the opponent's left lapel with my right hand and pull.
2. As the opponent resists by pulling back, I make use of his reaction to jump around behind him from his right side.
3. I then grasp his left shoulder from behind with my left hand and pull with both hands to apply a choke as I push with my forehead to the back of his head.

痛締 Itami-Jime

Tachi-Waza (Standing Technique).

1. With my right hand, I take a grip high on the opponent's left lapel with my thumb on the inside. With my left hand, I take a grip high on the opponent's right lapel with my thumb on the inside.
2. I then apply the choke by simultaneously pushing in with my thumb joints to the lymph nodes on both sides of his neck.

押締 Osae-Jime

Tachi-Waza (Standing Technique).

1. With my right hand, I take a grip high on the opponent's left collar with my thumb on the inside. With my left hand, I take a grip high on the opponent's right collar with my thumb on the inside.
2. I then push my thumb tips downward into Ryūmon on both sides of his neck to choke.

逆押締 Gyaku-Osae-Jime

Tachi-Waza (Standing Technique).

1. With my right hand, I take a grip high on the opponent's left collar with my thumb on the inside. With my left hand, I take a grip high on the opponent's right collar with my thumb on the inside.
2. I then push my thumb tips upward into the lymph nodes under the sides of his jawbone to choke.

坐締 Suwari-Jime

Suwari-Waza (Seated Technique).

1. I step forward with my right foot, grasp the opponent's left shoulder with my right hand and pull.
2. As the opponent resists by pulling back, I make use of his reaction to jump around behind him from his right side.
3. I then place my left arm behind his neck and apply Sankaku-jime.

15

TAKAGI YOSHIN RYŪ: CHŪDEN SABAKI GATA

中伝捌型

片胸捕 Katamune Dori

Tachi-Waza (Standing Technique).

1. The opponent grabs my left lapel with his right hand, which I cover by lightly placing my left hand on top of it.
2. As the opponent attempts to grab my right sleeve with his left hand, I step back with my left leg and drop to my left knee so as he falls on his back.
3. I then apply an armlock to the fallen opponent.

両胸捕 Ryōmune Dori

Tachi-Waza (Standing Technique).

1. The opponent grabs both my lapels, which I cover by lightly placing both my hands on top of his.
2. I then give a Kiai (a shout) and kick up to the opponent's groin with a right shin kick.
3. Finally, I apply a lock to the opponent's left wrist, step back with my left leg and drop to my left knee so as the opponent falls on his back.

鬼砕 Oni Kudaki

Tachi-Waza (Standing Technique).

1. The opponent attacks with a right punch.
2. I step diagonally back with my right foot and parry the attack with my left arm.
3. I then bring my right hand up from under the opponent's right arm, join hands with my left and apply Omote-Oni-Kudaki.
4. While maintaining the lock, I step in with my right foot and bring the opponent down with Ōsoto-Gake.

背負鎌 Seoi Gakari

Tachi-Waza (Standing Technique).

1. The opponent attacks with a right punch.
2. I step diagonally back with my right foot and parry the attack with my left arm.
3. I then bring my right hand up from under the opponent's right arm, join hands with my left and apply Oni-Kudaki.
4. Finally, I enter with my hips and throw the opponent forward with Ippon-Seoi-Nage.

腰投鎌 Koshi Nage Gakari

Tachi-Waza (Standing Technique).

1. The opponent grabs my right lapel with his left hand and attacks with a right punch.
2. I grasp the opponent's left elbow with my right hand and push it upwards from below as I step diagonally back with my right foot and parry his punch with my left hand.
3. I then enter with my right hip and throw him with Koshi-Nage.

腕折 Ude Ori

Tachi-Waza (Standing Technique).

1. The opponent grabs my left lapel with his right hand.

2. I lightly place the palm of my right hand on top of his grabbing hand and strike to Kasumi on the left side of his head with a left Ura-Shutō.
3. I then apply Ura-Gyaku to this right hand as I step back with my right foot and drop to my right knee, causing him to fall face down.
4. Finally, I place my left shin onto his right elbow and apply a lock.

逆手投 Gyakute Nage

Tachi-Waza (Standing Technique).

1. The opponent grabs my left lapel with his right hand.
2. I grasp his right hand from below with my left and push it upwards to capture his wrist in Omote-Take-Ori.
3. I then grasp the opponent's right armpit with my right hand and enter with my right hip to throw him.

鬼門投 Kimon Nage

Tachi-Waza (Standing Technique).

1. The opponent grabs both my lapels.
2. I grasp the opponent's armpits and push in with both thumb joints.
3. I then pull as I enter with my right hip and throw the opponent with Koshi-Nage.

当投 Ate Nage

Tachi-Waza (Standing Technique).

1. The opponent grabs my right lapel with his left hand.
2. I grasp his left hand from below with my right and push it upwards to capture his wrist in Omote-Take-Ori.
3. I then step under his left arm while maintaining the lock on his wrist, turn around, grasp his left armpit from behind with my left hand and pull him down onto his back.

小蝶捕 **Kochō Dori**

Tachi-Waza (Standing Technique).

1. The opponent grabs my right lapel with his left hand.
2. I control the opponent's elbow with both hands, turn to my left, bring his arm onto my right shoulder and throw him.

16

TAKAGI YOSHIN RYŪ: CHŪDEN TAI NO KATA

中伝体之型

腰車 Koshi Guruma

Tachi-Waza (Standing Technique).

1. The opponent grabs the front of my belt with his left hand, the back of my belt with his right, enters with his right hip and attempts to throw me.
2. I grasp the back of the opponent's belt with my left hand and strike to his face with my right.
3. I fall on my side, in front of the opponent, as I grasp his left ankle with my right hand and push upwards to throw him forwards with a Sutemi Waza (sacrifice throw).

四ツ手 Yotsude

Tachi-Waza (Standing Technique).

1. The opponent grabs my left shoulder with his right hand and the front of my belt with his left.
2. I match the opponent's grips by grasping his left shoulder with my right hand and the front of his belt with my left.
3. The opponent takes three steps back. I take three steps forward,

following his movement and maintaining the same distance throughout.
4. I then step in deeply with my left foot between his legs, place my right foot onto his left hip and throw him with Tomoe-Nage.

四ツ手崩 Yotsude Kuzushi

Tachi-Waza (Standing Technique).

1. The opponent grabs both my lapels.
2. I grasp the front of the opponent's belt with my left hand, his left shoulder with my right, step forward with my right foot and push.
3. Making use of the opponent's reaction, I then slide my left leg between his legs, place my right foot onto his left hip and throw him with Tomoe-Nage.

刑頭 Keito

Tachi-Waza (Standing Technique).

1. The opponent grabs my hair from behind with his right hand.
2. I grasp the opponent's right wrist with my left hand, lower my hips, take a step back with my left foot and turn to face him while standing ready to strike with my right fist.
3. The opponent then takes three steps back. I take three steps forward, following his movement and maintaining the same distance throughout.
4. On the last step, I jump to the opponent's left side, strike to his face with my right hand and throw him with Yoko-Tomoe-Nage.

腰折 Koshi Ori

Tachi-Waza (Standing Technique).

1. The opponent attempts to throw me with Koshi-Nage.
2. I strike to Suigetsu with my right fist, then grasp his left shoulder, also with the right hand as my left grasps the back of his belt.
3. Next, I step with my left foot in front of the opponent, place my right foot onto his left hip, pull with my right hand and throw him with Yoko-Tomoe-Nage.

腰流 **Koshi Nagare**

Tachi-Waza (Standing Technique).

1. The opponent grabs both my lapels.
2. I grasp his shoulders with both hands, slide both my feet to the outside of his left leg and throw him with Yoko-Nagare.

雲井返 **Kumoi Gaeshi**

Tachi-Waza (Standing Technique).

1. The opponent grabs both my lapels.
2. I grasp his left lapel with my left hand and his right lapel with my right and apply Gyaku-Jime.
3. While still applying the choke, I place my right foot on his left hip and throw him with Tomoe-Nage.

両手掛 **Ryōte Gake**

Tachi-Waza (Standing Technique).

1. The opponent grabs both my lapels.
2. I press with my thumbs into Hoshi-Shita on both his arms, place my right foot on his left hip and throw him with Tomoe-Nage.

水流 **Suiryū**

Tachi-Waza (Standing Technique).

1. The opponent grabs both my lapels.
2. I grasp the opponent's shoulders and slide my left foot between his legs as I slide my right foot to his left side.
3. I then pull the opponent's shoulders with both of my hands and throw him over the top of me.

柳雪 **Ryūsetsu**

Tachi-Waza (Standing Technique).

1. The opponent grabs both my lapels.

2. I grasp over the top of the opponent's left shoulder with my right hand and his upper right arm, near the shoulder joint, with my left.
3. I then place my right foot onto the opponent's left hip and slide my left foot between his legs to throw him with Yoko-Tomoe-Nage.

越後崩 Echigo Kuzushi

Tachi-Waza (Standing Technique).

1. The opponent grabs both my lapels.
2. I grasp the insides of the opponent's elbow joints with both hands and push upwards.
3. I then pull to strike to the opponent's face with my forehead, slide both my feet between his legs and throw him with Tachi-Nagare.

鵲 Kasasagi

Tachi-Waza (Standing Technique).

1. The opponent attacks from the side with Koshi-Nage.
2. I grasp the opponent's left shoulder with my right hand and the front of his belt with my left.
3. I then slide both my feet to his left side to throw him over the top of me with Yoko-Nagare.
4. I roll up on top of the opponent and apply a collar choke.

票墜 Hyōtsui

Tachi-Waza (Standing Technique).

1. The opponent grabs both my lapels.
2. I grasp both the opponent's shoulders, place my right foot on his left hip and throw him with Tomoe-Nage.
3. I follow the throw to roll up on top of him in Uma-Nori and apply a collar choke.

蔦搦 **Tsuta Garami**

Tachi-Waza (Standing Technique).

1. The opponent grabs both my lapels.
2. I grasp the opponent's sides, under his arms, and press in.
3. I then slide my feet to the opponent's right and throw him with Yoko-Tomoe-Nage.
4. I follow the throw to roll up on top of him in Uma-Nori and apply a collar choke.

瀧落 **Taki Otoshi**

Tachi-Waza (Standing Technique).

1. The opponent grabs both my lapels.
2. I grasp both the opponent's lapels, slide my feet between his legs and throw him with Tachi-Nage.
3. I follow the throw to roll up on top of him in Uma-Nori and apply a collar choke.

17

TAKAGI YOSHIN RYŪ: OKUDEN SHIRABE GATA

奥伝調型

梅吐 Ume Haki

1. I attack the opponent with Hon-Jime.
2. The opponent counters by grabbing my left lapel with his right hand while using his left hand to push my left wrist to his right.
3. As I then turn in for a right-side Seoi-Nage, the opponent blocks my throw.
4. I follow up by wrapping my right arm over his right arm, wrapping my right leg around the inside of his right leg and taking him down on his back with Ko-Uchi-Gake.
5. I finally hold him down and apply a collar choke.

車返 Kuruma Gaeshi

1. The opponent attacks with either Hon-Jime or Gyaku-Jime.
2. I grasp the opponent's sides with both hands and twist to apply pain.
3. I then place my right foot on the opponent's left hip and throw him with Tomoe-Nage.

天返 Ten Gaeshi

1. The opponent attempts to throw me with Seoi-Nage.
2. I grasp the left side of his belt from behind with my left hand, the front of his belt with my right and leap over him to fall at his feet.
3. As the opponent is thrown over me, I deliver a punch with my right hand that is holding his belt.

流捕 Nagare Dori

1. The opponent grabs my left lapel with his right hand.
2. I grasp the opponent's right wrist with my left hand and bring my right arm up from below his right elbow to pull his arm in for Te-Makura.
3. I fall back while applying Te-Makura, maintaining the lock on his right elbow.

山落 Yama Otoshi

1. The opponent grabs my left lapel with his right hand and my right sleeve with his left. I grasp the opponent's sleeve and lapel in the same manner.
2. I then apply Omote-Gyaku to the opponent's right hand with my left, as I bring my right arm over his right arm to wrap it up and apply a lock to his right elbow.
3. Next, while maintaining the lock on the opponent's right arm, I slide my right foot to my left with Yoko-Nagare, causing the opponent to fall on his back.
4. From this position on the ground, I tighten the lock on the opponent's right arm.

靹嵐 Tomo Arashi

1. The opponent grabs my left lapel with his right hand and my right sleeve with his left. I grasp the opponent's sleeve and lapel in the same manner.
2. I then step in deeply with my right foot, rotate my right arm under the opponent's left armpit, turn my hips in and take him straight down with Ganseki-Otoshi.

袖車 Sode Guruma

1. The opponent grabs my left lapel with his right hand and my right sleeve with his left. I grasp the opponent's sleeve and lapel in the same manner.
2. I then step in deeply to the opponent's right side with my left foot, push up from below his left elbow with my right hand and throw him with Ōsoto-Nage.

両手掛 Ryote Gake

1. The opponent grabs my left lapel with his right hand and my right sleeve with his left. I grasp the opponent's sleeve and lapel in the same manner.
2. I rotate my right hand around to grasp the opponent's left wrist, then bring my left arm over his left arm to wrap it up and apply a lock to his right elbow from above.
3. Finally, I step back with my left foot and drop to my left knee as I apply pressure to the opponent's left elbow joint with my left arm, causing him to fall face down.

肝砕 Kimo Kudaki

1. The opponent grabs my left lapel with his right hand and my right sleeve with his left. I grasp the opponent's sleeve and lapel in the same manner.
2. I rotate my right arm under and around the opponent's left arm to capture it with Musō-Dori
3. I then push down to Matsu-Kaze with my left hand as I step back with my right foot to drop to my right knee, causing the opponent to fall on his back.

雷落 Rai Raku

1. The opponent grabs my left lapel with his right hand and my right sleeve with his left. I grasp the opponent's sleeve and lapel in the same manner.
2. I rotate my left arm over and around the opponent's right arm from above to capture it with Musha-Dori.

3. I then grasp the opponent's right shoulder with my right hand, step in deeply to his right side with my left foot and throw him with Ōsoto-Gake while maintaining the lock on his right arm.

体砕 Tai Kudaki

1. The opponent grabs my left lapel with his right hand and my right sleeve with his left. I grasp the opponent's sleeve and lapel in the same manner.
2. I step in deeply with my left foot to the opponent's right side and place my hips in position to throw him with Ōsoto-Nage.
3. I then drop to my left knee to throw, causing the opponent to fall straight down onto the back of his head.

想風 Sofū

1. The opponent grabs both my lapels.
2. I also grasp the opponent's lapels, push into the sides of his neck with both thumbs and strike to his face with my forehead.
3. While maintaining the grip, I drop to place my back on the floor and both my feet on the opponent's hips to throw him with Tomoe-Nage.
4. Finally, I roll up on top of the opponent and apply a collar choke.

逆捕 Gyaku Dori

1. The opponent grabs my right lapel with his left hand and punches with his right.
2. I parry the strike with my left and lift the opponent's left hand high in Omote-Take-Ori.
3. I then step in with my right foot as I grab the opponent's right arm with my left to throw him with Seoi-Nage, while still maintaining the lock on his left wrist.

乱風 Rampu

1. The opponent attacks by grabbing my left lapel with his right hand and the front of my belt with his left.
2. I grasp the opponent's right lapel with my left hand and his left armpit with my right.
3. I then step in deeply with my right foot, rotate my hips in and throw the opponent forward while maintaining the same grips.

風雪 Fūsetsu

1. The opponent grabs my lapels with both hands and attempts to apply a collar choke. I grasp his sides with both hands and twist to apply pain.
2. I then step in deeply with my left foot to his right side and throw him with Ōsoto-Nage.

18

TAKAGI YOSHIN RYŪ: OKUDEN MOGURI GATA

奥伝潜型

極楽落 Gokuraku Otoshi

1. The opponent grabs my left lapel with his right hand and my right sleeve with his left. I grasp the opponent's sleeve and lapel in the same manner.
2. I rotate my right arm under and around the opponent's left arm from the outside and grasp his sleeve just above his elbow joint.
3. I then step back with my right foot and pull with my right arm.
4. I clasp my left hand together with my right, push down on the opponent's left elbow joint to reinforce the lock and take a step back with my left foot.
5. Finally, I enter with my hips and use the opponent's left arm to throw him with Ganseki-Nage.

地獄捕 Jigoku Dori

1. The opponent grabs my left lapel with his right hand and my right sleeve with his left. I grasp the opponent's sleeve and lapel in the same manner.
2. I rotate my right arm under and around the opponent's left arm from the outside and grasp his sleeve just above his elbow joint.
3. I then step back with my right foot and pull with my right arm.

4. I clasp my left hand together with my right, push down on the opponent's left elbow joint to reinforce the lock.
5. Finally, I place my left foot behind the opponent's left foot and take him down backwards with Ōsoto-Gake while maintaining the lock on his left elbow.

玉砕 Tama Kudaki

1. The opponent grabs my lapels to apply Hon-Jime.
2. I grasp the opponent's sides with my hands and press in at the pressure point on his left side with my right thumb.
3. As the opponent then turns his body diagonally to his left to escape the pain, I enter with my right hip to throw him with Koshi-Nage.

飛鳥捕 Hichō Dori

1. The opponent attacks with a right-handed strike to the left side of my head.
2. I parry the attack with my right arm, then use my right hand to push his right wrist away to my left.
3. As the opponent tenses his arm to resist his hand being pushed away, I leap in and throw him with Katate-Nage.

鬼伏 Oni Buse

1. The opponent grabs my left lapel with his right hand and my right sleeve with his left. I grasp the opponent's sleeve and lapel in the same manner.
2. I place my left hand lightly on the opponent's right hand and press with my left thumb to the pressure point on his little finger.
3. The opponent attempts to pull his right hand back from the pain.
4. I follow his pull, push up under his jaw with my right hand and take him down with Ōsoto-Gake.

稲妻捕 Inazuma Dori

1. The opponent grabs my left lapel with his right hand and my right sleeve with his left. I grasp the opponent's sleeve and lapel in the same manner.
2. I wrap the opponent's left arm up from below with my right hand, tighten the lock, then twist to my left as I drop to my left knee and throw him.

水鳥 Mizu Tori

1. The opponent grabs my left lapel with his right hand and my right sleeve with his left. I grasp the opponent's sleeve and lapel in the same manner.
2. I wrap the opponent's left arm up from below with my right hand and tighten the lock.
3. I then press to Matsu Kaze with my left hand, step diagonally back with my right foot and drop to my right knee to take the opponent down onto his back.
4. I hold the opponent down (Osaekomi).

来雪 Kuru Yuki

1. The opponent grabs my left lapel with his right hand and my right sleeve with his left. I grasp the opponent's sleeve and lapel in the same manner.
2. I turn diagonally to my left and wrap my left hand up and over the opponent's right arm from below.
3. I then step between the opponent's legs with my right foot and throw him with Koshi-Nage.

体落 Tai Otoshi

1. The opponent grabs my left lapel with his right hand and my right sleeve with his left. I grasp the opponent's sleeve and lapel in the same manner.
2. I strike with a right punch, turn to face diagonally to my left and enter with my right foot for Uchi-Mata.
3. The opponent blocks my throw, wraps his right hand around my

left arm from the outside, steps in with his left foot and enters
with his hips in an attempt to throw me with Koshi-Nage.

4. I counter by dropping to my right knee to take the opponent
   straight down on his back.

潜捕 Moguri Dori

1. The opponent grabs my left lapel with his right hand and my right
   sleeve with his left. I grasp the opponent's sleeve and lapel in the
   same manner.
2. I strike with a right punch, turn to face diagonally to my left and
   enter with my right foot for Uchi-Mata.
3. The opponent blocks my throw, wraps his right hand around my
   left arm from the outside, steps in with his left foot and enters
   with his hips in an attempt to throw me with Koshi-Nage.
4. I counter by dropping to my right knee as I also grasp the
   opponent's right shoulder with my right hand to pull him down.
5. I hold the opponent down (Osaekomi).

潜投 Moguri Nage

1. The opponent grabs my left lapel with his right hand and my right
   sleeve with his left. I grasp the opponent's sleeve and lapel in the
   same manner.
2. I wrap up the opponent's right arm from the outside and grasp the
   pressure point on his right side with my right hand.
3. I then enter with my hips and use the opponent's right arm to
   throw him with Seoi-Nage as I drop to my left knee.

19

TAKAGI YOSHIN RYŪ: MUTŌ DORI GATA
無刀捕型

拳者捕 Kenja Dori

1. I am in Ichimonji no Kamae. The opponent cuts down from Daijōdan no Kamae with a Daitō (long sword).
2. I turn to my left, sliding my right foot around to align my feet. The opponent's cut flows past on my right side.
3. I grasp the opponent's right wrist with my left hand and strike to the back of his hand with a right punch.
4. I then immediately follow up with a right punch to his upper left arm, causing the opponent to release the sword.
5. Next, I place my right thumb on the back of the opponent's right hand and step back with my left foot to apply Omote-Gyaku, causing the opponent to fall on his back.
6. I pick up the fallen sword and maintain Zanshin (a state of alertness).

一文字 Ichimonji

1. I am in Hira Ichimonji no Kamae. The opponent cuts down from Daijōdan no Kamae with a Daitō.
2. As the opponent cuts, I step in deeply with my right foot, drop to my left knee and strike to Suigetsu with my right hand.

3. The opponent is knocked down onto his back.
4. I withdraw while maintaining Zanshin.

柄落 Tsuka Otoshi

1. I am in Seigan no Kamae, with my right hand extended in front of me and my left hand at my upper right lapel. The opponent holds his Daitō in Daijōdan no Kamae.
2. I leap in to stop his elbows with my hands by pushing upwards.
3. I then step in front of the opponent's right foot with my right and grasp the Kojiri (pommel) with my right hand, pushing upwards and entering in with my hip to throw him.
4. I take the opponent's sword as he is flipped onto his back.

向捕 Mukō Dori

1. I am in Seigan no Kamae. The opponent cuts down from Daijōdan no Kamae with a Daitō.
2. I evade by taking a step to my left and control the opponent's sword by grasping the opponent's right wrist with my left hand.
3. I then grab the Kojiri (pommel) from above with my right hand and pull upwards as I strike to the opponent's face with my left.
4. If the opponent doesn't fall from the strike, I cut up from his groin as I take the opponent's sword from his grip.

廻捕 Mawashi Dori

1. I am in Gedan no Kamae, with my right hand in front, my left hand at my upper left lapel and my hips low. The opponent cuts down from Daijōdan no Kamae with a Daitō.
2. I turn to my left and use the edge of my right hand to strike to the opponent's right forearm. I then follow up by kicking to the opponent's left wrist with my right foot causing him to release the sword.
3. Next, I press to the opponent's Adam's apple with my right hand as I sweep his legs with my right foot to throw him with Ōsoto-Gake.
4. The opponent falls on his back. I pick up the sword and maintain Zanshin.

後捕 Ushiro Dori

1. I am in Hira Ichimonji no Kamae. The opponent thrusts in from Seigan no Kamae with a Daitō.
2. I turn to my left and kick up at the opponent's right hand with my right foot. I then leap behind him and simultaneously strike to both his ears with Happa-Ken.
3. The opponent is knocked unconscious and falls down. I withdraw maintaining Zanshin.

沈捕 Shizumi Dori

1. I lower my hips into Gedan no Kamae. The opponent thrusts in from Seigan no Kamae with a Daitō, then changes to cut horizontally to my right side.
2. I evade his attacks, then step in from my right to stand directly in front of the opponent.
3. I grasp the opponent's left wrist with my left hand and push it up high.
4. I then step in and drop to my knee as I thrust my right hand up at his groin to throw him forward (Omote-Nage).

20

TAKAGI YOSHIN RYŪ: DAISHO SABAKI GATA

大小捌型

柄砕 Tsuka Kudaki

1. I stand facing the opponent. The opponent is wearing Daisho (long and short swords) thrust in his belt, with his right hand on the hilt of his Daitō (long sword).
2. I press down on the Tsuka-Gashira (pommel) of the opponent's sword with my right hand as I strike to his wrist with a left Shutō.
3. I then kick up at his groin with my right foot as I draw his sword.

引捕 Hiki Dori

1. I stand facing the opponent. The opponent attempts to draw his Daitō.
2. I strike to both the opponent's forearms with my hands, then draw his sword with my right and take up a position to stab.

入捕 Iri Dori

1. The opponent stands in Daijōdan no Kamae with a Daitō. I am in Hira Ichimonji no Kamae.
2. As the opponent cuts down, I step in deeply with my right foot, drop to my left knee and strike to Suigetsu with my right hand.

3. I then grasp the hilt of the opponent's Shotō (short sword) and pull to draw it.
4. Finally, I thrust in to stab with the Shotō.

乱岳 Rangaku

1. The opponent walks forward wearing Daisho thrust in his belt. I follow close behind him.
2. I grasp the end of his Saya (scabbard) from behind with my left hand and his left wrist with my right.
3. The opponent places his hand on the Tsuka (handle) of his Daitō.
4. As he attempts to draw his sword, I bar his left elbow with the Saya from behind as the Tsuka of his sword scoops up from the inside of his left leg.
5. Finally, I push down on the Saya with my left hand, holding the opponent down with the lock.

掬捕 Sukui Dori

1. The opponent attempts to draw his Daitō.
2. I kick up at the opponent's right hand with my right foot in time with his draw, knocking the sword from his grasp.
3. I then step forward before the opponent can recover to draw his Shotō and deliver a right-hand strike to the end of his nose.
4. Finally, I draw his Shotō with my left and thrust in with the blade.

桝骨 Masubone

1. The opponent cuts down from Daijōdan no Kamae with a Daitō.
2. I step back with my right foot to evade. The cut flows past my right side.
3. I grasp the opponent's right wrist with my left hand and strike with my right elbow to the opponent's face.
4. I remove the sword from his grip and deliver a horizontal cut as if I am casting his sword away.

潮返 Ushio Gaeshi

1. The opponent cuts down from Daijōdan no Kamae with a Daitō.
2. I step back with my right foot to evade. The cut flows past my right side.
3. I grasp the opponent's right arm with my left hand and strike to his right forearm with a right Shutō causing him to drop his sword.
4. I then leap in, strike to Jinchū with my right hand and take him down with Ōsoto-Gake.

掛落 Kake Otoshi

1. The opponent holds his Daitō in Daijōdan no Kamae.
2. I leap in to press up against the opponent's elbows with both hands.
3. As he takes a step back, I deliver a shin kick to his groin while pushing up against the Kojiri (pommel) of the sword with my right hand.
4. Finally, I strike to Tentō with the back of his blade, causing him to fall.

小手止 Kote Dome

1. The opponent cuts down from Daijōdan no Kamae with a Daitō.
2. I evade diagonally to my left. The opponent's sword flows past on my right side.
3. I grasp the opponent's right hand in Omote-Gyaku with my left and bring my right hand up to meet it.
4. I then turn to my left, drop to my left knee and throw the opponent with Omote-Gyaku.

横刀 Yoko Gatana

1. The opponent places his hand on his Daitō.
2. I press up from below the Tsuka (handle) with my right hand.
3. As the opponent takes a step back, I strike to Suigetsu with my right elbow as I draw his sword with my left hand, then sweep the sword back for a horizontal cut.

車投 Kuruma Nage

1. The opponent places his hand on his Daitō.
2. I press up from below the Tsuka (handle) with my right hand.
3. As the opponent takes a step back, I strike to Suigetsu with my right elbow.
4. Next, I place my right hand on the opponent's left hip and fall to the side to throw him with Yoko-Nagare.
5. As the opponent is thrown over, I grab the Tsuka of the opponent's Daitō with my left hand so that he is disarmed as he is thrown.
6. Finally, I roll to a standing position and deliver a cut to the opponent.

四ツ手刀 Yotsude Gatana

1. The opponent places his hand on his Daitō.
2. I press down on the Tsuka (handle) of the opponent's Daitō with my right hand, grasp the Tsuka of his Shotō with my left hand and stomp down to Kyokei with my right foot.
3. As the opponent steps back, his Shotō is drawn by my left hand and I thrust in with the blade.

刃結 Yaiba Musubi

1. The opponent places his hand on his Daitō.
2. I grasp the Tsuka (handle) of the opponent's Shotō with my right hand and press down on the Tsuba (sword guard) of his Daitō.
3. As the opponent takes a step back, his Shotō is drawn and I deliver a horizontal cut.

透捕 Sukashi Dori

1. The opponent cuts down from Daijōdan no Kamae with a Daitō.
2. I evade by turning to my left.
3. The opponent follows up with a horizontal cut.
4. I jump back to escape.
5. I then leap in and strike to Suigetsu with my right fist.
6. As the opponent winces, I throw him with Koshi-Nage.

GYOKKO RYŪ
KOSSHIJUTSU

玉虎流骨指術

21

GYOKKO RYŪ: JŌ RYAKU NO MAKI

上略之巻

虚空 Kokū

1. The opponent attacks with a right punch to the face.
2. I parry the attack with my left hand, then follow up with a right Shutō to Hoshi-Shita on the opponent's right arm.
3. The opponent follows up with a right kick.
4. I kick up from below his right leg with my left foot, then strike to Butsumetsu with my left thumb.

輦與 Renyo

1. The opponent attacks with a right punch to the face, I parry the attack with my left hand.
2. The opponent kicks with his right foot, I evade to the outside and kick up from below with my right foot.
3. The opponent then grabs my left lapel with his right hand.
4. I strike to Amado on the right side of the opponent's neck with a right Shutō, then grasp his right hand with my right apply Ura-Gyaku as I step to my right.
5. As I perceive the opponent to look down, I grasp the inside of his right elbow with my left hand and pull.
6. I then turn the opponent's right hand around in a large motion to

my left with Omote-Gyaku, as I kick with my right foot, knocking the opponent to the ground on his back.
7. Finally, I kick down to the chest of the fallen opponent with my left foot.

弾手 Danshu

1. The opponent grabs my right sleeve with his left hand.
2. I pull my right elbow back as I rotate my right hand anticlockwise to capture the opponent's left arm in Musō-Dori.
3. The opponent then attacks with a right punch. I parry with my left arm and follow up with a strike to Amado on the left side of the opponent's neck with a left Shutō.
4. I then deliver a right kick to the opponent's left knee joint as I tighten the lock on his left arm with my right, causing him to fall on his back.
5. Finally, I kick down to the opponent's side with my right foot.

弾指 Danshi

1. The opponent grabs my right lapel with his left hand. I hold the opponent's grabbing hand with my right in the form of Omote-Gyaku.
2. The opponent then follows up with a right punch to my face.
3. I parry the attack with my left arm and immediately follow up with a strike to the opponent's chest with my left thumb.
4. Next, I tighten the Omote-Gyaku lock on the opponent's wrist with my right hand as I kick to his left knee joint with my right foot, causing the opponent to fall on his back.
5. Finally, I kick down to the fallen opponent's chest with my right foot.

逆流 Gyaku Nagare

1. The opponent attacks with a right punch.
2. I step diagonally to my left and parry with my right arm.
3. The opponent attacks with a right kick.
4. I counter by kicking up from below his right leg while catching his right hand in Omote-Gyaku.

5. The opponent then attacks with a left punch to my solar plexus.
6. I parry the attack with my right arm, strike to Amado on the right side of the opponent's neck with a right Shutō and tighten the Omote-Gyaku on his right hand, causing the opponent to fall on his back.
7. Finally, I kick down to the fallen opponent with my right foot.

鳧鷗 Keō

1. The opponent grabs my lapels with both hands.
2. I deliver a right shin kick to the opponent's groin, then strike down with both hands to his arms from above to break his grip.
3. The opponent attacks with a right punch.
4. I parry the attack with my left hand, then strike with a right Shutō to Kasumi.
5. Finally, I deliver a right kick to the opponent's chest to knock him down and withdraw while maintaining Zanshin (a state of alertness).

跳火 Hanebi

1. The opponent grabs my collar at the back of my neck from behind.
2. I turn to my left, lower my hips and place the palm of my right hand on the back of the opponent's grabbing hand, with my fingers wrapping around the edge of it.
3. The opponent attacks with a right kick.
4. I parry the opponent's kick with the outside of my left arm, take the opponent's right hand in Ura-Gyaku with my right, press down to tighten the lock, then turn my body and kick with my right foot, as I apply Omote-Gyaku to take the opponent down on his back.

闕倒 Ketō

1. The opponent attacks with a right kick.
2. I step back with my left foot and deliver a right kick to the opponent's kicking leg from below.
3. The opponent attacks with a right punch.
4. I parry with my left arm, strike to the opponent's face with a right

Shako-Ken, then follow up with a right kick to the opponent's chest to knock him down.

5. I withdraw maintaining Zanshin.

指砕 Yubi Kudaki

1. The opponent grabs my collar at the back of my neck from behind.
2. I turn to my left, lower my hips and place the palm of my right hand on the back of the opponent's grabbing hand, with my fingers wrapping around the edge of it.
3. The opponent pulls back, creating an opening, in which I enter while striking to the opponent's chest with my left hand and taking his right hand in Ura-Gyaku.
4. I then step back with my left leg and drop to my left knee to take the opponent down on his back.
5. Finally, I kick down to the opponent with my right foot.

締脈 Ketsu Myaku

1. The opponent attacks with Sankaku-Jime from behind.
2. I lower my hips and hold the opponent's right arm lightly with my left hand as I apply pain to the inside of his right elbow joint with my right thumb.
3. I then throw the opponent with Ippon-Seoi-Nage.
4. I finish by kicking down to the opponent with my right foot.

殺締 Saketsu

1. The opponent attacks with Kannuki-Jime (bear hug) from behind me. I respond by pushing my hips back to create an opening.
2. I then apply a lock to the fingers of opponent's right hand with my right hand as I turn to my right to strike back at the opponent's face with my left hand and throw him forwards with Ganseki-Otoshi.
3. I finish by kicking down to the opponent with my right foot.

蹄拳 Teiken

1. The opponent attacks with Hagai-Jime (full nelson) from behind me. I counter by lowering my hips as I spread my arms out wide.
2. I grasp both of the opponent's hands and apply a lock to each of them, with my thumbs applying pressure to the backs of his hands. I open his arms wide and slip out to my left, underneath his left arm.
3. Then, using only my right hand, I throw him with Katate-Nage.
4. I finish by kicking down to the opponent with my right foot.

22

GYOKKO RYŪ: CHŪ RYAKU NO MAKI

中略之巻

鳥鵲 Ujaku

1. The opponent attacks with a right punch to the face.
2. I step to my left to evade, as I parry the attack with my right arm, grasp the opponent's sleeve and pull.
3. The opponent attacks with a right kick.
4. I evade and parry the attack with a right kick to the side of his kicking leg.
5. I then lift the opponent's right arm high and strike to his right side with my left thumb.
6. I step under the opponent's right arm, coming out to his left side and grasp his right wrist with my left hand to throw him with Katate-Nage.
7. Finally, I kick down to the opponent with my right foot.

鯖倒 Seitō

1. The opponent attacks with a right punch to the face.
2. I step diagonally to my right and parry the attack with my left hand.
3. The opponent kicks with his right foot, I step diagonally to my left and parry the kick with my right hand.

4. The opponent follows up with a left punch to the solar plexus.
5. I evade to the outside of the attack, parry the opponent's punch with my left hand and grasp his wrist.
6. I then strike to the opponent's face with a right Shako-Ken, grab his shoulder with my right hand, kick with my right foot to his left leg, step back with my right foot and drop to my right knee, causing the opponent to fall on his back.
7. I finish by kicking down to the fallen opponent with my right foot.

拏振 Dashin

1. The opponent attacks with a right-hand stab with a Shōtō (short sword).
2. I evade to my left and grasp the opponent's right wrist with my left hand.
3. I then strike to the back of the opponent's right hand with my right to knock the blade out of his grip.
4. The opponent attacks with a left kick.
5. I kick up from below with my right foot to the opponent's kicking leg and take his right wrist in Omote-Gyaku, as I step back with my left foot to throw him.
6. Finally, I kick down to the opponent with my right foot.

虚落 Koryaku

1. The opponent cuts down from above with a Shōtō.
2. I step back diagonally with my left foot, turning my body to parry with my right arm and grasp the opponent's wrist.
3. I then strike with a left Shutō to Kasumi on the right side of the opponent's head.
4. The opponent tries to pull his right hand from my grip, I go with the pull and step under his right arm, coming out on his left side to throw him with Katate-Nage.
5. Finally, I kick down to the opponent with my right foot.

蜂先 Hōsen

1. The opponent cuts down diagonally from his right with a Shōtō.
2. I evade the cut by stepping back diagonally with my left foot,

lower my hips and kick to the opponent's right arm with my right
foot, knocking the blade from his grip.

3. I then thrust down to the opponent's throat with three fingers of
   my right hand to knock him down on his back.
4. Finally, I kick down with my right foot to the opponent's chest.

樺 Kō

1. The opponent cuts down from above with a Shōtō.
2. I evade the attack by stepping diagonally to my right, parrying
   with my left arm and grasping his sleeve.
3. The opponent attacks with a right kick.
4. I lower my hips and scoop up under the kick with my right arm to
   the outside of the opponent's right leg to catch it, as I pull on his
   right arm, causing him to fall on his back.

獅猿 Shien

1. The opponent attacks with a stab from behind with a Shōtō.
2. I evade by stepping back with my left foot and grasping the
   opponent's right wrist as it flows past on my right side.
3. The opponent attacks with a right kick.
4. I evade to the outside of the opponent's attack and kick up from
   below to the opponent's right leg with my right foot.
5. I then apply Omote-Gyaku to the opponent's right wrist with both
   hands as I step back with my left foot and drop to my left knee as
   I turn to my left to throw the opponent.
6. Finally, I kick down to the fallen opponent with my right foot.

崩落 Hōraku

1. The opponent cuts down from behind with a Shōtō.
2. I step back with my left foot and grab the opponent's right wrist
   with my right hand.
3. I then step to my right as I bring my right arm over the
   opponent's right arm, to catch behind his right elbow, and apply
   Take-Ori to his right wrist with my left hand, forcing him to
   release the Shōtō.

4. While keeping the opponent's wrist in a lock with my left hand, I strike to his face with a right Shutō.
5. I grasp the opponent's right shoulder with my right hand, place my right foot behind his right foot and drop to my left knee as I pull, to take the opponent down on his back.
6. Finally, I kick down to the opponent with my right foot.

23

GYOKKO RYŪ: GE RYAKU NO MAKI

下略之卷

隼雄 **Shunu**

1. As the opponent attempts to draw his Daitō (long sword), I move in and control the Tsuka-Gashira (pommel) of his sword with my left hand.
2. The opponent takes one step back to again attempt to draw his Daitō.
3. I follow the opponent's movement by stepping forward, and thrust under his nose with my right thumb, causing him to step back once more.
4. As he retreats, I grasp the Tsuka-Gashira with my right hand as I also step back, to draw the sword.
5. With my right hand holding the Tsuka-Gashira, I grasp the back of the sword blade with my left and stand ready to thrust with the sword.

隼足 **Shunsoku**

1. As the opponent attempts to draw his Daitō, I move in and control the Tsuka-Gashira (pommel) of his sword with my left hand.
2. The opponent then attempts to strike to my left wrist with his

right.

3. I release my left-hand grip to evade the opponent's strike and turn to the opponent's left side, grasping the end of the opponent's Saya (scabbard) with my right hand and his left wrist with my left hand.
4. I lift and turn over the Saya with my right hand, using it to lock the opponent's left elbow and causing him to fall face down.
5. I kick to the fallen opponent and hold him down with the arm lock applied to his left elbow with the Saya.

一撃 Ichi Geki

1. At the moment the opponent lifts his Daitō into Daijōdan no Kamae, I leap in to control his right elbow with my left hand and strike to his chest with my right thumb.
2. As the opponent's balance is taken momentarily backward, I follow up with a right kick to his chest, knocking him down.
3. Finally, I deliver a right kick to the side of the fallen opponent's right knee.

魁足 Kaisoku

1. The opponent cuts down from Daijōdan no Kamae with a Daitō.
2. I turn my body to my left to evade the cut, which flows past the right side of my body, as I deliver a right kick to the opponent's right hand, knocking the sword out of his grip.
3. The opponent then grasps his Shōtō (short sword). I strike with a right Shutō to Kasumi on the right side of the opponent's head.
4. As the opponent flinches, I grab his right elbow with my left hand and use my right foot to throw him with Ōsoto-Nage.

掬掠 Koraku

1. The opponent cuts down from Daijōdan no Kamae with a Daitō.
2. I evade the cut by taking a step to my right with my right foot.
3. As the opponent's sword flows past on my left side, I grab his right wrist with my left hand, wrap up his right elbow by scooping my right arm from below and dropping down to throw the opponent forwards with Te-Makura.

4. I roll up to a standing position while maintaining Zanshin (a state of alertness).

意合封 Iai Fū

1. The opponent lets out a Kiai (a shout) as he draws his Daitō to cut horizontally to my right side. I leap back to evade.
2. As the opponent then lifts his Daitō into Daijōdan no Kamae, I leap in to control his elbows and block his downward cut with my left arm, as I strike to the left side of his chest with my right thumb.
3. I then deliver a right kick to knock the opponent over and withdraw while maintaining Zanshin.

沈雁 Chingan

1. The opponent stands in Seigan no Kamae with a Daitō. I am in Bansetsu no Kamae.
2. As the opponent attacks with a straight thrust to my chest, I evade by turning to my left and lowering my hips. The opponent's stab flows past my right side as I grasp the opponent's right wrist with my left hand.
3. I then bring my right hand to the back of the opponent's right as I lower my hips and turn the sword to overhead to my left, pulling my left leg back and dropping to my left knee to throw the opponent with Omote-Gyaku.
4. Finally, I kick down to the opponent with my right foot.

風孟 Fū

1. The opponent cuts down from Daijōdan no Kamae with a Daitō.
2. I evade to my left as I hook the fingers of my right hand over the top of the opponent's Tsuba (sword guard).
3. I then simultaneously strike with a left Shutō to the opponent's face, as I pull with my right hand to remove the sword from his grip.
4. Finally, I grasp the Tsuka (handle) of the sword with my left hand and deliver a horizontal cut to the opponent to fell him.

KOTŌ RYŪ KOPPŌJUTSU

虎倒流骨法術

KOTŌ RYŪ: KURAI DORI
位取

右正眼之構 Migi Seigan no Kamae

I stand facing the opponent with my feet apart, my right hand held straight out in front and my left hand in a Shutō, touching my right shoulder.

左正眼之構 Hidari Seigan no Kamae

I stand facing the opponent with my feet apart, my left hand held straight out in front and my right hand in a Shutō, touching my left shoulder.

平一文字之構 Hira Ichimonji no Kamae

I am standing upright with my hands extended out to either side in a straight line.

抱圍之構 Hōkō no Kamae

I am standing with both my hands open, held at the height of my face and my hips low.

防備之構　Bōbi no Kamae

I am standing upright with my right fist extended in front of me and my left hand held in a fist at my hip.

KOTŌ RYŪ: SHODEN GATA
初伝型

抒投 Yokutō

1. The opponent grabs my left sleeve with his right hand and my right lapel with his left.
2. I strike to Yūgasumi with the tip of my right thumb, then deliver a right shin kick to the opponent's groin.
3. Finally, I strike up under the opponent's jaw with my left palm to knock him down.

押虚 Ōgyaku

1. The opponent attempts to throw me with a right Koshi-Nage.
2. I block the throw by pulling my right elbow back, lowering my body weight and rolling my left thumb into Shichibatsu.
3. I then strike to Butsumetsu with my right hand to knock the opponent down.

抗抒 Kōyoku

1. The opponent attacks with a right punch to the face.
2. I parry the attack with my left arm and then strike to Ura-Kimon with my right fist.

3. Finally, I bring my left arm from under the opponent's right arm to throw him with Ganseki-Nage.

拡倒 **Shitō**

1. The opponent grabs both my lapels and attempts to apply a collar choke.
2. I counter by striking to Kasumi with the thumb joint of my right hand.
3. I then step back with my left foot, turn to my left and apply Omote-Gyaku to the opponent's right wrist while simultaneously applying pressure to the back of this right hand with my left thumb.

捕捉 **Hosoku**

1. The opponent grabs my right lapel with his left hand, then attacks with a right punch.
2. I parry the opponent's attack with my left arm, then strike to Koe with my right thumb as I simultaneously strike to the opponent's face with my forehead, knocking him down.

放擲 **Hōteki**

1. The opponent grabs my right lapel with his left hand, then attacks with a right punch.
2. I parry by striking to Hoshi-Shita with a left Shutō, knocking the opponent's attack up and away.
3. I then place my right thumb to Hoshi on the opponent's left arm and push upward, creating space to enter with my right hip and throw him with Koshi-Nage.

斜倒 **Shatō**

1. The opponent grabs my right lapel with his left hand, then attacks with a right punch.
2. I parry the attack with my left hand, then strike to Yūgasumi with my right thumb before delivering a right shin kick to Suzu, knocking the opponent down.

掛倒 **Ketō**

1. The opponent grabs both my lapels.
2. I step back with my right foot and strike to the inside of the opponent's wrists from above with both fists to break his grip.
3. Next, utilising the momentum of the step back, I swing my right leg up to kick with the sole of my right foot to Gorin, knocking the opponent down.

搾撃 **Sakugeki**

1. The opponent attempts to grab both my lapels.
2. I strike up to Asagasumi with my right thumb, then kick sideways with the instep of my right foot to Kaku on the opponent's right leg to knock him down.

擔撃 **Tangeki**

1. The opponent attacks with a left, then right punch.
2. I step back diagonally with my left foot and I parry the opponent's left punch with my right arm, then lower my hips and lift both my arms to Hōkō no Kamae (also known as Gantsubushi no Kamae) to receive the opponent's right punch. This is Kyo (feint / deception). The Jitsu (actuality) is that I deliver a right kick with the sole of my foot to Suigetsu, knocking the opponent down.

拔技 **Batsugi**

1. The opponent grabs my left lapel with his right hand.
2. I push the joint of my left thumb into the back of the opponent's right hand as I apply Omote-Gyaku.
3. I then step forward and strike with the fingertips of my right hand to the left side of the opponent's face, knocking him down.

折倒 **Settō**

1. The opponent grabs my left lapel with his right hand.
2. I punch sideways to Jyakkin on the opponent's grabbing arm with

my right fist, followed by a strike to Butsumetsu with the tip of my left thumb to knock him down.

指拍 **Shihaku**

1. The opponent attacks with a left, then right punch.
2. I step back diagonally with my left foot and parry the opponent's left punch with my right arm, then take a large step back diagonally with my right foot and parry the opponent's right punch with my left arm.
3. I feign that I will kick to Suzu with my right foot, this is Kyo (feint / deception). The Jitsu (actuality) is that I deliver a right-hand strike to In / Kage.

拒技 **Kyogi**

1. The opponent attacks with a left, then right punch.
2. I step back diagonally with my left foot and parry the opponent's left punch with my right arm, then step back diagonally with my right foot and parry the opponent's right punch with my left arm.
3. I stomp down with my right foot to Toki on the opponent's right foot followed by a punch to In / Kage with my right fist.

括拷 **Kakkō**

1. The opponent attacks with a left, then right punch.
2. I step back diagonally with my left foot and parry the opponent's left punch with my right arm, then step back diagonally with my right foot and parry the opponent's right punch with my left arm.
3. I deliver a kick with the instep of my right foot to Sai on the inside of the opponent's right leg.
4. I then place the fingers of my right hand to the point Matsu-Kaze and thrust the opponent down in one movement.

浦波 **Uranami**

1. The opponent attacks with a left, then right punch.
2. I parry the attacks, then deliver a right kick to Yaku on the inside of the opponent's right leg.

3. I strike with the thumbs of both hands simultaneously to Amado on both sides of the opponent's neck.

天地 Tenchi

1. The opponent attacks with a left, then right punch.
2. I step back diagonally with my left foot and parry the opponent's left punch with my right arm, then step back diagonally with my right foot and parry the opponent's right punch with my left arm.
3. I deliver a right toe kick to Suzu, then strike to the left side of the opponent's face with the five fingers of my right hand.

片巻 Katamaki

1. The opponent attacks with a right, then left punch.
2. I parry both attacks, then enter in to wrap the opponent's left arm clockwise from the outside with my right arm.
3. I strike to Butsumetsu with my left thumb, as I turn to my right to take the opponent down.

26

KOTŌ RYŪ: CHŪDEN GATA
中伝型

飛打 Hida

1. The opponent and I stand facing each other.
2. I strike with a right Shutō to Kasumi, then knock the opponent down with a right toe kick to Suzu.
3. I step back with my right foot and maintain Zanshin (a state of alertness).

飛搾 Hisaku

1. The opponent and I stand facing each other.
2. I strike to Amado on the left side of the opponent's neck with my right thumb tip, then jump up to scissor the opponent's torso with both my legs.
3. Next, I drop my shoulders to the ground and use both my hands to grasp the opponent's ankles and pull, so that he falls on his back.
4. I apply the leg-lock Ami-Jime to the opponent's right achilles.

Figure 2.26.1: Ami-Jime

飛鳥 Hichō

1. The opponent and I stand facing each other.
2. I strike to the left side of the opponent's face with the five fingers of my right hand, then kick to In / Kage with my right foot.
3. I withdraw and maintain Zanshin.

飛倒 Hitō

1. The opponent and I stand facing each other.
2. I strike to Ura-Kimon with three fingers of my right hand, then jump up and kick to Butsumetsu with both feet.
3. I land with both my hands touching the tatami and roll once to return to my original standing position.

括飛 Kappi

1. The opponent approaches.
2. I strike to the right Amado with a right Shutō, then make a small hop on the spot to switch my feet and strike to the left Amado with a left Shutō.
3. I leap back to retreat.

押飛 Monpi

1. The opponent approaches.
2. I grasp the left side of the opponent's body with the fingers of my right hand and twist as my thumb presses into Butsumetsu.
3. I then deliver a right kick to Koe on the opponent's right leg to knock him down. I withdraw and maintain Zanshin.

夊倒 **Suitō**

1. The opponent attacks with a left, then right punch.
2. I parry the attacks, then leap away to escape.
3. The opponent leaps in, grasps my left wrist and attempts to throw me with Koshi-Nage.
4. I lower my hips to block the opponent's throw. I then strike to Butsumetsu on the left side of the opponent's body with my right elbow, followed by a strike to the opponent's face with the back of my right fist.
5. I grasp the hand that is holding my wrist with my left hand, lower my hips and place my right foot in front to the opponent to throw him with Koshi-Nage.

顧飛 **Gohi**

1. The opponent approaches.
2. I press down at the point Matsu-Kaze with the fingers of my right hand. This strike resembles a cat scratching and therefore is known as Nezumi Tori (catching a mouse).
3. I then strike up to Asagasumi with the palm of my left hand to knock the opponent down.

撤飛 **Hetsubi**

1. The opponent approaches.
2. I press down at the point Matsu-Kaze with the fingers of my right hand.
3. I then thrust with the five fingers of my left hand to the opponent's face and escape by leaping sideways a distance of Ikken (1.8m).

擲返 **Tekigaeshi**

1. The opponent approaches.
2. I thrust up with my right thumb into the opponent's left armpit, in front of his arm joint, then kick to Sai on the opponent's left leg with the instep of my right foot and withdraw.

喉倒 Kōtō

1. The opponent approaches.
2. I press down at the point Matsu-Kaze with the fingers of my right hand.
3. I kick to Suzu with my left foot to knock the opponent down.

攪飛 Kakuhi

1. The opponent grasps my lapels with both hands.
2. I strike up to Asagasumi with my right hand, then deliver a right kick to the opponent's inner thigh to thrust him down.

27

KOTŌ RYŪ: OKUDEN NO KATA
奥伝之型

攅当 Santō

1. The opponent leaps in and grabs my left lapel with his right hand and my right sleeve with his left hand. He then uses his right leg in an attempt to throw me with Uchi-Mata.
2. I counter by striking down from above with my right fist to Kaku on the inside of the opponent's right leg as I simultaneously strike up from below with my left fist to Hoshi-Shita on the opponent's right arm.
3. I withdraw back a step, maintaining Zanshin.

攅倒 Santō

1. I am in Seigan no Kamae. The opponent attacks with a straight thrust to my chest with a Shōtō (short sword).
2. I shift my centre of gravity to my left foot and lower my hips to evade the attack.
3. As the opponent's stab flows past my right side, I grasp his right wrist that is holding the Shōtō with my left hand and strike to Hoshi-Shita with the fingers of my right hand.
4. I then hold the opponent's right hand in Omote-Gyaku, as I step

in with my right foot and deliver a right punch to the back of his right hand, knocking the blade from his grip.

5. Next, I apply pressure to the back of the opponent's hand, held in Omote-Gyaku with my right thumb, as I turn to my right and deliver a left kick to Sai on the opponent's left leg to thrust him down in one movement.

虎倒 Kotō

1. The opponent cuts down from above with a Shōtō.
2. I leap in with my left foot to bring it in front of the opponent's right foot and deliver a left strike to Hoshi-Shita on the opponent's right arm.
3. I then strike to both the opponent's ears with my left and right palms simultaneously with Happa-Ken.
4. I follow up with a right shin kick to Suzu.

神剪 Shinsen

1. The opponent grasps both my lapels and attempts to choke me.
2. I strike to both the opponent's ears simultaneously with Happa-Ken, then use my forehead to strike directly to the opponent's face.

梱飛 Konpi

1. The opponent is poised to attack.
2. I take a step forward with my left foot to place it in front of the opponent's right foot as I strike to Amado with a left Shutō.
3. I then leap away to my right.

挈摺 Josetsu

1. The opponent approaches.
2. I turn my body diagonally to my right as I strike to Jujiro with my right hand.
3. I then deliver a right kick to Gorin to knock the opponent down.

抓摺 Sōsetsu

1. The opponent approaches.
2. I grasp the opponent's sides with both hands and press to Butsumetsu with both thumbs.
3. Using my grip to twist his body diagonally to my left, I step diagonally backward with my left leg to my right and drop to my left knee to throw the opponent.

抓倒 Sōtō

1. The opponent approaches.
2. I grasp each side of the opponent's upper collar with both hands, push down with both thumbs and pull to strike to his face with my forehead.
3. I then place my right foot at the opponent's hip joint to throw him with Tomoe-Nage.
4. I roll over with the opponent to take the position Uma-Nori and choke.

扣鬼 Kōki

1. The opponent approaches.
2. I strike to both the opponent's ears with Happa-Ken.
3. I jump up to kick with both feet to Suigetsu and use the recoil from the kick to somersault back to a standing position.

This technique can also be performed by striking to Amado with the right hand then kicking with both feet to Suigetsu while executing a somersault back to a standing position.

鬼門 Kimon

1. The opponent approaches.
2. I grasp under the opponent's armpit with my right hand and push to Kimon with my thumb.
3. I then enter with my hip, step back with my left leg and drop to my left knee to throw the opponent.

乱雪 Ransetsu

1. The opponent approaches.
2. I grasp under the opponent's armpit with my right hand and push to Kimon with my thumb.
3. I then slide between the opponent's legs with both feet to throw him with Tachi-Nagare, causing him to strike his head on the ground.

This technique can also be performed with Yoko-Nagare to the left or right.

裏鬼門 Ura Kimon

1. The opponent approaches.
2. I make it look as if I will grab the opponent's lapel with my right hand, but I actually strike to Gorin with five fingers.
3. I then kick to Gorin on the opponent's abdomen with my right foot to knock him down.

28

KOTŌ RYŪ: HEKITŌ GATA

劈刀型

蹴朴 **Sokuboku**

1. The opponent is in Daijōdan no Kamae with a Daitō (long sword). I am in Migi Seigan no Kamae.
2. As the opponent cuts down to the top of my head, I evade by turning my body to face to my right and deliver a right kick to Hoshi-Shita on the opponent's right arm.
3. The opponent's sword is knocked out of his hands and I enter, striking to his face with the five fingers of my right hand to knock him down.

朴返 **Bokuhen**

1. As Kyo (deception), I drop to the ground and roll backwards once.
2. The opponent holds a Daitō in Chūdan no Kamae. I am in Hei-Ichimonji no Kamae.
3. The opponent cuts to the right side of my body. I leap diagonally back to my left with my right foot to evade.
4. As the opponent then moves to Daijōdan, I leap in and control Hoshi-Shita with my right hand as I deliver a right kick to Suigetsu to knock him down.

打扣 **Dakō**

1. The opponent holds a Daitō in Chūdan no Kamae. I am in Hōkō no Kamae.
2. The opponent thrusts at my chest with the sword. I evade by cross-stepping forty-five degrees forward with my right foot to bring it in front of the opponent's right foot.
3. I grasp the opponent's right wrist with my left hand in Omote-Gyaku and deliver a right punch to the back of his right hand, causing him to release his sword.
4. I then step to my right and I turn my body, drop to my left knee and apply Omote-Gyaku to the opponent's right hand, taking him down on his back.

手力 **Shuriki**

1. The opponent holds a Daitō in Daijōdan no Kamae. I am in Bōbi no Kamae.
2. As the opponent cuts down, I step forward, turning to my right and in the flow of the opponent's attack, I strike with a right hand Shutō to his arms, causing him to release the sword.
3. I then follow up with a right hand Shutō across the bridge of the opponent's nose.

跂望 **Kibō**

1. The opponent holds a Daitō in Daijōdan no Kamae. I am in Hidari Seigan no Kamae.
2. As the opponent cuts, I step to my right, turn my body and punch strongly to Jakkotsu from the side.
3. I then deliver a right kick to Butsumetsu to knock the opponent down.

跋扈 **Bakko**

1. The opponent holds a Daitō in Chūdan no Kamae. I am in Bōbi no Kamae.
2. The opponent cuts to my right side. I step forward and turn my

body diagonally to my left as I strike with my right hand to Jinchū to knock the opponent down.

跖力 Sekiryoku

1. The opponent holds a Daitō in Daijōdan no Kamae. I am in Hōkō no Kamae.
2. The opponent cuts down from Daijōdan. I step forward with my right foot, as I drop to my left knee and strike to Suigetsu with my right fist, knocking the opponent down.

跨飛 Kahi

1. The opponent holds a Daitō in Chūdan no Kamae. I am in Hei Ichimonji no Kamae.
2. The opponent thrusts at my chest with the sword. I evade by stepping back with my right foot in a big motion and turning my body to face my right.
3. The opponent then cuts horizontally at the right side of my body. I step forward in front of the opponent and drop down low, placing both my hands on the ground, to evade the opponent's cut.
4. Once the opponent's cut passes over the top of me, I jump up to kick to Suigetsu with both feet, knocking the opponent down.

29

KOTŌ RYŪ: KAIDEN GATA
皆伝型

悟心 Goshin

1. The opponent approaches.
2. I turn sideways and retreat by leaping backwards. I neither attack him nor try to flee, which will cause the opponent to act hastily.
3. When he hurriedly leaps in to attack, I can strike to an easy target such as Amado, Kirigasumi, Kimon or Butsumetsu, knocking him down in one blow.

一念 Ichinen

1. The opponent approaches.
2. I stare at the opponent's face as if looking into his eyes, but I am actually fixing my eyes on his eyelashes.
3. The opponent feels himself frozen in place and is unable to close in on me as I use Isshin Ichinen (mental focus) to freeze him in place with Ganshin Ichijyo Fudomi (lit. Eyes and mind in unison, immovable body).

活眼 **Katsugan**

1. In the case of an opponent approaching in the dark of night, I lower my hips and, rather than looking for the person, I look for any movement of air and throw Senban Shuriken in that direction.
2. In the case of finding myself surrounded by multiple opponent's during the daytime, I throw Senban Shuriken in all eight directions.
3. The way to throw Senban Shuriken is to place the index finger to the front of the Shuriken, the middle, ring and little fingers below and use the wrist action to spin them forward. The wrist is aimed towards the opponent.

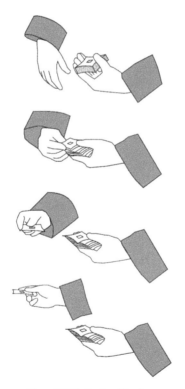

Figure 2.29.1: Senban Shuriken

TOGAKURE RYŪ NINPŌ TAIJUTSU

戸隠流忍法体術

30

TOGAKURE RYŪ: TAIJUTSU UKEMI GATA

体術受身型

The following Kata are performed while wearing 手鈎 *Shukō (hand claws).*

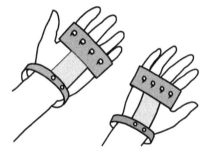

Figure 2.30.1: Shukō

返し鳥 Kaeshi Dori

1. The opponent cuts down with a Daitō (long sword) from Daijōdan no Kamae.
2. I drop down low and place both my hands on the ground to evade the opponent's cut.
3. I then leap up, kick to Suigetsu with both my feet and somersault backward to a standing position.

拳流 Ken Nagashi

1. The opponent cuts down from Daijōdan no Kamae with a Daitō.
2. I step in with my right foot as I drop to my left knee and deliver a right-hand strike to Suigetsu.
3. I then roll away and return to a standing position.

一之構 Ichi no Kamae

1. I stand in Ichi no Kamae. I hold off the opponent by turning my body sideways and extending my left hand forward. My right hand is held open at my left shoulder and my bodyweight is divided between my feet.
2. As the opponent then strikes in, I evade as I parry and counter with either hand.

一刀捕 Ittō Dori

1. The opponent holds a Daitō in Daijōdan no Kamae.
2. I stand in Ichi no Kamae with my right side forward.
3. As the opponent cuts down, I use the Shukō to block with the palm of my left hand as my right hand strikes to the opponent's face.
4. I then bring my right hand down to grip the back of the opponent's sword, twist my hands to lock the Shukō to the blade, and step back with my right foot while turning my body to remove the Daitō from the opponent's grip.

横蹴 Yoko Geri

1. The opponent holds a Daitō in Seigan no Kamae, I am in Hira Ichimonji no Kamae.
2. As the opponent attacks with a straight thrust at my chest, I lower my hips, shift to my left and kick up to the opponent's hands from below with my right foot, knocking the sword out of his grip.
3. I then strike to Suigetsu with my right hand.

一刀斬 Ittō Giri

1. The opponent holds a Daitō in Daijōdan no Kamae.
2. I hold a Daitō in Seigan no Kamae.
3. As the opponent cuts in, I lower my hips and evade to my left as I cut upwards with my sword to the right side of the opponent's body.

31

TOGAKURE RYŪ: SHINOBI GAESHI GATA
忍返型

重返 Shige-Gaeshi

1. I am standing outside of a wall encircling a building as the opponent approaches.
2. I place both of my hands on the wall, lift my left elbow up on top and pull with my right hand, using the reaction to swing my body onto the wall into a sideways facing position.

重捕 Shige-Tori

1. I am standing outside a wall encircling a building as the opponent approaches.
2. I place both of my hands on the wall, lift my left elbow up on top and pull with my right hand, using the reaction to swing my body onto the wall in a sideways facing position.
3. From the sideways facing position, as the opponent reaches the wall below me, I swing my legs back to kick at this face with both feet. I then leap inside the compound and roll away.

空飛 **Sora-Tobi**

1. I jump up to place my foot on the trunk or one of the thick lower branches of a tree and spring up two or more branches to grab a higher branch with my left hand to pull myself up.
2. I then grasp the trunk of the tree with my legs, allowing me to throw Senban Shuriken with my right hand.

横流 **Yoko-Nagare**

1. An opponent to the front holds a Tachi (long sword) in Daijōdan no Kamae and an opponent to the rear holds a Yari (spear) in Chūdan no Kamae.
2. When I sense the moment that their Sakki (killing intent) is at its most intense, I give a Kiai and throw Metsubushi (blinding powder) with my right hand as I roll to my left with Yoko-Nagare.

後流 **Ushiro-Nagare**

1. Three opponent's approach from the front armed with Tachi and Yari.
2. I throw Metsubushi to the front as I roll silently to the rear with Ushiro-Nagare and escape.

中返 **Chū-Gaeri**

1. The opponent approaches from the rear.
2. I execute Chū-Gaeri (somersault) to escape.

In the beginning, practice Chū-Gaeri by first placing your hands on the ground in front, then work up to being able to perform Chū-Gaeri without using your hands.

横返 **Yoko-Gaeri**

1. The opponent approaches from the rear.
2. I execute Chū-Gaeri to the side (cartwheel) to escape.

飛違 Tobi-Chigai

1. The opponent approaches.
2. I execute a Chū-Gaeri, leap up to the trunk of a large tree and use Shūko to climb.

一刀投 Ittō-Nage

1. The opponent approaches
2. I draw my sword and throw it directly at him.

鉄盤投 Teppan-Nage

1. In my left hand I hold nine Senban Shuriken, my right hand takes them one by one and throws them from my left side, sideways, directly at the opponent.
2. I line up the opponent with my right wrist as I throw them with the feeling of a wrist flick. *(Refer to Figure 2.29.1)*

切返 Kiri-Kaeshi

1. The opponent stands in Daijōdan no Kamae with a Daitō (long sword).
2. I hold my Daitō in Chūdan no Kamae.
3. I harmonise with both, the Kiai and the attacking cut of the opponent, as I thrust out while rolling my wrists to cut into his body.

捨身 Sutemi

1. I am facing multiple opponents.
2. I first feign a straight thrust at the strongest opponent, then cut at the weakest in the group to break through their cordon and escape.

32

TOGAKURE RYŪ: SANTŌ TONKŌ NO KATA

竄逃遁甲の型

When preparing for a demonstration with these Kata, you should sew two pockets on the inside of your jacket's left lapel, one to conceal Metsubushi (blinding powder) and the other to conceal practice Shuriken (rubber, wood or paper).

The following Kata also employ the Goton no Tonkei (Five form of escape) of Moku-ton (wood escape), Ka-ton (fire escape), Do-ton (earth escape), Kin-ton (metal escape) and Sui-ton (water escape).

片腕遁走型 Kata-Ude Tonso-Gata

1. The opponent grabs my right wrist with his right hand and pulls.
2. With my right wrist in the opponent's grasp, I step forward to go with the first, then second pull.
3. On the third pull, I lift the opponent's right wrist high in Take-Ori and kick to his groin with my right foot.
4. I rotate to my left, under the opponent's arm to throw him with Katate-Nage.
5. I then throw Metsubushi and leap away to hide using Do-Ton.

左右遁走型 Sayū Tonso-Gata

1. The opponent grabs my left wrist with his right hand and pulls.
2. I step forward to go with the first, then second pull.

3. On the third pull I lift the opponent's right wrist up high by applying Take-Ori with my left hand.
4. My right hand then grasps the opponent's right arm; I kick to his groin with my right foot, step back with my right leg and drop to my right knee to take the opponent face down to the ground.
5. I throw Metsubushi and leap away to hide using Do-Ton.

首筋遁走型 Kubi-Sugi Tonso-Gata

1. As I walk forward, the opponent grabs the back of my collar with his right hand to stop me.
2. The opponent pulls me backward and I step with the first, then second pull.
3. On the third pull, I lightly place my right hand on the opponent's right, strike to Suigetsu with my left elbow, apply a lock to the opponent's right hand and throw him with Katate-Nage.
4. Finally, I throw Metsubushi and leap away to hide using Moku-Ton.

当込遁走型 Ate-Komi Tonso-Gata

1. The opponent stands with a Daitō in Daijōdan no Kamae. I am in Hachimonji no Kamae, with my hips low, my left hand extended straight in front of me in a Shutō and my right hand in front of my right shoulder with my right thumb extended upwards.
2. I give a Kiai at the opponent then leap in to strike to Suigetsu with my right thumb, leap away to my right side, throw Metsubushi and escape using Moku-Ton.

小手打遁走型 Kote-Uchi Tonso-Gata

1. The opponent stands with a Daitō in Daijōdan no Kamae. I am in Hachimonji no Kamae.
2. The opponent cuts down. I evade to my left side and strike to the opponent's forearm with a right Shutō, causing him to drop his sword.
3. I then follow up with a right punch to the opponent's left side, which knocks him down.

4. Finally, I throw Metsubushi, leap to my left and escape using Moku-Ton.

右打遁走型 Migi-Uchi Tonso-Gata

1. The opponent stands with a Daitō in Seigan no Kamae. I am in Happō no Kamae.
2. The opponent gives a Kiai and attacks with a straight thrust at my chest with a Daitō. I evade the attack by turning to my right and striking with a right Shutō to the opponent's forearm.
3. I then grasp the Tsuka (handle) of his sword with my left hand and pull to remove it from him.
4. Finally, I throw Metsubushi with my right hand as I leap away to my right and escape using Moku-Ton.

左右雲隠型 Sayū Kumogakure-Gata

1. Two opponents with Daitō, held in Daijōdan no Kamae, approach from either side of me at a distance of around 4 metres.
2. I am in Happō-Gakure no Kamae with my hips low, both my hands are held above my head concealing Metsubushi and my legs are apart in a wide stance.
3. Both opponents move in towards me with the intention of cutting down. I retreat two or three steps, then throw the Metsubushi directly at them with both my hands.
4. I leap in and strike with my thumbs, then execute two Chū-Gaeri (somersaults) and escape using Moku-Ton.

攻勢霧隠型 Kosei Kirigakure kata

1. Four opponents approach me from a distance of four or five meters away with Daitō held in Daijōdan and Seigan no Kamae. I am in Tonso no Kamae, with my right foot in front and my left foot behind me in a posture that shows an intention to flee.
2. In my left hand I hold the number of Teppan Shuriken equal to the number of opponent's I am facing.
3. As the opponents attack, I throw the shuriken causing them to flinch.

4. I leap in, throwing Metsubushi, execute Chū-Gaeri between the opponents in front of me and escape using Moku-Ton.

八方霧隠型 **Happo Kirigakure Kata**

1. Three opponents are in front of me and two are behind me.
2. I step forward and throw Teppan Shuriken at the opponents in front. As the opponents behind me move to cut, I throw Metsubushi behind me.
3. I leap through an opening between the opponents and escape using Moku-Ton.

BIBLIOGRAPHY

Hatsumi, M. (2019), *Jinsei Mutō Dori*. Tokyo: Japan Publications Inc.

Hatsumi, M. (2018), *Ninjutsu Kyōden: Taijutsu*. Tokyo: BAB Japan.

Hatsumi, M. (2018), *Ninjutsu Kyōden: Bukijutsu*. Tokyo: BAB Japan.

Hatsumi, M. (2014), *The Complete Ninja: The Secret World Revealed*. Tokyo: Kodansha.

Hatsumi, M. (2013), *Ninpo Taizen* Tokyo: Kodansha.

Hatsumi, M. (2008), *The Unarmed Fighting Techniques of the Samurai*. New York: Kodansha.

Hatsumi, M. (2006), *Japanese Sword Fighting: Secrets of the Samurai*. Tokyo: Kodansha.

Hatsumi, M. (2005), *Advanced Stick Fighting*. Tokyo: Kodansha.

Hatsumi, M. (2004), *The Way of the Ninja: Secret Techniques*. Tokyo: Kodansha.

Hatsumi, M. (1991), *Hiden Ninja Submission*. Tokyo: Keibunsha

Hatsumi, M. (1988), *Essence of Ninjutsu: the Nine Traditions*. Chicago Contemporary Books.

Hatsumi, M. (1988), *The Grandmaster's Book of Ninja Training*. Chicago Contemporary Books.

Hatsumi, M. and Hayes, S. (1987), *Ninja Secrets from the Grandmaster*. Chicago Contemporary Books.

Hatsumi, M. (1987), *Sekai-no Martial Arts (Martial Arts of the World)*. Tokyo: Tsuchiya Shoten

Hatsumi, M. (1986), *Sōjutsu*. Tokyo: Tsuchiya Shoten

Hatsumi, M. (1986), *Bōjutsu*. Tokyo: Tsuchiya Shoten

Hatsumi, M. (1983), *Togakure Ryū Ninpō Taijutsu*. Tokyo: Shin Jinbutsu Oraisha

Hatsumi, M. (1983), *Knife / Pistol Fighting*. Tokyo: Tsuchiya Shoten

Hatsumi, M. (1983), *Hanbō / Jutte / Tessen*. Tokyo: Tsuchiya Shoten

Hatsumi, M. (1981), *Ninjutsu - History and Tradition*. Burbank, CA. Unique Publications

Hatsumi, M. (1981), *Ima Ninja*. Tokyo: Chobunsha

Hatsumi, M. (1978), *Sengoku Ninpō Zukan*. Tokyo: Shin Jinbutsu Oraisha

Hatsumi, M. (1975), *Hiden Togakure Ryū*. Tokyo: Tsuchiya Shoten

Hatsumi, M. and Chambers, Q. (1971), *Stick Fighting - Techniques of Self-Defence*. Tokyo: Kodansha

BUJINKAN PERIODICALS

Bujinkan Densho Sanmyaku (1990 to 1995). Eleven Issues

Bujin (1989). Nine Issues

Tetsuzan (1988 to 1989). Six Issues

ABOUT THE AUTHOR AND ILLUSTRATOR

Duncan Mitchell has trained in Bujinkan Dōjō Budō Taijutsu for over three decades and has been an instructor since 1995. His Dōjō, the Budō Dōkōkai, has been conducting martial arts classes in Brisbane since 1997, organised seminars for visiting senior instructors and hosted several large training events.

Duncan lived and trained in Japan from 1990 to 1995, where he studied directly under the grandmaster Masaaki Hatsumi-sensei and senior Bujinkan instructor Isamu Shiraishi-sensei. He continues to return to Japan yearly to further his study in the martial arts of Japan.

- Awarded 5th Dan and Shidoshi (Instructor) Rank: 1995
- Awarded with the Bujinkan Gold Medal: 2001
- Awarded the highest Dan rank issued in the Bujinkan: 2009
- Received the Būfū Ikkan Shin-Gi-Tai Award: 2011
- Awarded Yūshū Shihan: 2015
- Awarded Dai-Shihan: 2017

Duncan has spent his working life as a draftsman, both in Japan and Australia, and is currently living in Brisbane with his wife Yoshie. This is Duncan's first book.

Duncan can be contacted by email on: budodokokai@gmail.com,

At his website: www.budodokokai.com,

Or on the social media listed below:

facebook.com/budodokokai
twitter.com/BudoDokokai